Malcolm Doney grew up under the flight path for Heathrow Airport.
He studied Fine Art at Saint Martin's School of Art – now Central Saint Martin's UAL – before pursuing a career in journalism, advertising and broadcasting. He has written ten books, including, with his wife Meryl, *Who Made Me?*, a sex guide for seven year olds. They road-tested the book and have two children. He is a regular contributor to BBC Radio 2's *Pause for Thought*, and Radio 4's *Something Understood*. He lives in a village on the Suffolk coast where he keeps sheep and chickens, and is a volunteer priest in his parish church, sometimes joined by his horse, Neville.

Martin Wroe travelled to Wales in the womb of his mother because his father wanted him to be born Welsh. He is married to Meg, a painter, and together they have been raised by three children. He got into journalism while studying theology and ended up on the staff of the *Independent* and later the *Observer*. He has had longtime collaborations with an arts festival called Greenbelt, a human rights NGO called the Amos Trust and a band called U2. He is a sometime contributor to BBC Radio 4's *Thought for the Day* and volunteers as a priest in the Church of England, in North London. He was late to understand that religions are poems and tries to write one most days.

Praise for *Lifelines*

'A great guide full of clear, simple and useful wisdom on how to live and lovely reminders of what we too often forget.'
Matt Haig
Bestselling author of The Humans *and* How To Stop Time

'This book feels like balm to my weary heart. It's beautiful, wise, and, maybe most importantly, playful. The photos and essays make me think and make me smile. The authors know how to meet people where they are. Now my plan is to randomly pick a page every morning and see what challenges the universe is laying at my feet.'
Brené Brown
Research professor and author of the New York Times *#1 bestseller* Braving the Wilderness

'Lifelines is about those things in life we cannot see, that might change how we view the things we can. A book of faith for those wary of religion. Sacred text for the more earthy reader.'
Bono

'I really like this very fine book, with its wonderful combination of hard-won wisdom, creative images and memorable quotes. Makes me think it will find a lot of readers and a lot of YES.'
Richard Rohr
OFM, Franciscan, writer and speaker

'A handbook for those searching for meaning and reflecting on their place in the world. Totally accessible yet unafraid to handle the toughest of questions and topics, the book is visually beautiful. This book can be accessed by anyone and can be opened at any point and a pearl of wisdom found, dive in and submerge yourself or merely dip your toe.'
Rev. Kate Bottley
BBC Radio 2 presenter and Gogglebox *vicar*

'I love this book! For its inclusivity and directness. For taking religion by the horns. For mining wisdom from poetry, song, art, film, philosophy, history and theology, celebrating the convergence of ideas on how to live an inspired and inspiring life. For its bold illustrations and quotations. For its capacity to imagine a better world. For anyone who thinks 'Love is a verb' and 'The best things in life are not things'.'
Patience Agbabi
Spoken word poet and author of Telling Tales

'A wonderfully rich collection of insightful, inspiring and humorous reflections, and visually stunning too. Like a bag of Opal Fruits, it's hard to choose just one page and put it down. You can dip in, but then the next page, and the next, offers more enticing, juicy, thought-provoking stuff.'
Nick Park
Oscar-winning director and creator of Wallace and Gromit

'This book is equal parts challenging, profound and generous. It does not judge or condescend but instead talks to us with the ease and charm of an old friend. It demonstrates the rigour of hope and how we may find it in small ways. It manages to be breathtakingly bold in scope and still incredibly readable. There is much insight within these pages that I hope to return to again and again.'
Vanessa Kisuule,
Poet, performer and Bristol City Poet 2018 – 2022

'A book of calm, humane and good-humoured meditations, each like a small pool to be dipped into briefly for a rinse and a rest and a steadying of the nerves for the onward journey.'
Tim Winton
Novelist, twice shortlisted for the Booker

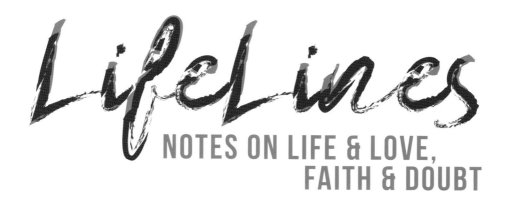

LifeLines

NOTES ON LIFE & LOVE, FAITH & DOUBT

MALCOLM DONEY & MARTIN WROE

DESIGN BY SIMON GUNN

Unbound

This edition first published in 2018

Unbound
6th Floor Mutual House, 70 Conduit Street, London W1S 2GF

www.unbound.com

Designed by Simon Gunn

A CIP record for this book is available from the British Library

ISBN 978-1-78352-627-7 (trade hbk)
ISBN 978-1-78352-629-1 (ebook)
ISBN 978-1-78352-628-4 (limited edition)

Printed in Barcelona by Novoprint

1 3 5 7 9 8 6 4 2

For

Ellie, Evan, Grace, Lewis and Wes

Over to you

Dear Reader,

The book you are holding came about in a rather different way to most others. It was funded directly by readers through a new website: Unbound. Unbound is the creation of three writers. We started the company because we believed there had to be a better deal for both writers and readers. On the Unbound website, authors share the ideas for the books they want to write directly with readers. If enough of you support the book by pledging for it in advance, we produce a beautifully bound special subscribers' edition and distribute a regular edition and ebook wherever books are sold, in shops and online.

This new way of publishing is actually a very old idea (Samuel Johnson funded his dictionary this way). We're just using the internet to build each writer a network of patrons. At the back of this book, you'll find the names of all the people who made it happen.

Publishing in this way means readers are no longer just passive consumers of the books they buy, and authors are free to write the books they really want. They get a much fairer return too – half the profits their books generate, rather than a tiny percentage of the cover price.

If you're not yet a subscriber, we hope that you'll want to join our publishing revolution and have your name listed in one of our books in the future. To get you started, here is a £5 discount on your first pledge. Just visit unbound.com, make your pledge and type **Lifelines5** in the promo code box when you check out.

Thank you for your support,

Dan, Justin and John
Founders, Unbound

CONTENTS

What does a good life look like and where can I get one?

There's nothing novel about this question, but the answer remains as elusive as ever. When questions about the meaning of life are answered convincingly, we're quite likely not to notice. That's because the 'answer' comes as often from the exemplary lives of shining individuals as it does from the advice of books or the words of teachers.

Still, every day we're surrounded by questions as old as the human race, and the clues we find in one generation may not resonate so much with the next:

Why is there something rather than nothing?

What is this thing called love?

Why am I sometimes such a bastard?

Why did she have to get sick?

How come music makes me cry?

... come to think of it, what's this life all about?

For a few thousand years, we might have looked to find answers to questions such as these in churches or synagogues, in mosques or temples. The great households of religion often claimed to have a monopoly on truth.

But then more and more of us stopped believing in them, stopped belonging to them.

Today, many of us don't really do religion like that. We may be fine sitting in the tranquility of some ancient house of prayer, but we'll probably slip off if anything resembling a service begins. We don't like to be told what to believe. We're shy of certainty, suspicious of authority.

Sometimes institutional religion itself seems to obscure the truths it lays claim to, worrying that people might interpret them in their own way, in their own lives. The gatekeepers of the faith traditions lose sleep over the terrifying prospect of their brand being diluted. It can feel like they'd rather keep people out than invite them in; that their preoccupations and anxieties are not those of the rest of us. This rigidity was summed up by the singer and activist Bono: 'In the war between the church and God, sadly, the church is winning.'[1]

But if many of us feel disconnected from formal religion, still we retain a longing for some deeper, richer narrative by which to navigate our days. We're inveterately curious, and open to ideas. We haven't closed the door on life's strange mysteries. How the big moments – the birth of a child, say, or the death of a friend – can leave us wondering about how to live in the small moments.

How to forgive someone.

If love is worth it.

What is enough?

Why people pray.

The authors of this book (that's us) have grown up in quirky, generous, god-haunted backgrounds and, if we've shed a few convictions over the years, we've picked up one or two others. None is stronger than a sense that *how we live* is more important than *what we believe*. And what we talk about when we talk about faith are the kind of field notes for living a good life that we've scribbled down in these pages. Perhaps there's another way of talking about this stuff, a different vocabulary.

In these lifelines we're often holding on to the wisdom of others: artists and activists, poets and songwriters, thinkers and dreamers. Some of them can reach out and touch faith, others feel like they never grasped it. This is less of a 'how to' book than a 'try this' book. It's more about clues and pointers than terms and conditions. It's

about how we might try to live well in this beautiful but baffling world.

Please don't feel you need to start at the beginning and plough through to the end. It's more of a dip-in-and-out thing. But if each spread stands alone, we hope that it's more than the sum of its parts. Less of an instruction manual, more of a sketch book. These are not the kind of lifelines that you might throw to someone who's fallen overboard, they're more lines about life that might help navigate the choppy seas.

In case you're counting, we've come up with 99 lines. Maybe you're thinking that's because, in Islam, there's a tradition that there are 99 names of Allah. Actually, it's probably that 99 is a number that seems reassuringly incomplete. Unfinished. There's always room for more.

There's another tradition, that Persian rug-makers and Amish quilt-stitchers put a deliberate mistake into their creations out of humility, because only God is capable of perfection. We may have done this too, but most of our errors are less deliberate.

We're following Leonard Cohen's advice to give up on the 'perfect offering' because 'there's a crack in everything.' Hopefully, as he added, 'That's how the light gets in.'[2]

You Don't Have To Choose Between Religion and Spirituality

Religion has an image problem. This might have something to do with its patriarchy. Or its homophobia. Or its elitism. It could be about being sectarian and exclusive – allied to an inability to update its theological software, which, on its worst days, leads to schism and violence. Religion has been responsible for most of the wars in history, claim its critics, but for all that, it's pretty resilient. As the American TV presenter Jon Stewart says: 'It's given people hope in a world torn apart by religion.'[1]

Is it religion's style that's the problem? Or its content? Or that general enduring sense of impenetrability? Whatever it is, for many people religion no longer ticks their boxes.

Spirituality, on the other hand, does.

Spirituality does not have the same image problem. Unlike religion, spirituality is soft, not hard. Fluid not fixed. It's about personal development and individual choice. If religion seems to be about guilt, duty and obligation, spirituality feels like its about growth and maturity. You have to fit into a religion but spirituality can be customised – it will fit in with you.

No wonder, as the comedian Lenny Bruce said, 'Every day people are straying away from the church and going back to God.'[2]

But maybe religion doesn't deserve such a bad rap. On its good days, religion stands up against power, and violence, and sides with the weak against the strong. It feeds the hungry, and teaches people to read and write. It inspires social movements that transform history for good. On its best days, religion produces the likes of Francis of Assisi, Dorothy Day, Martin Luther King and Marilynne Robinson.

It inspires heartbreaking music, powerful images, extraordinary buildings and wonderful stories. Its rites and rituals remind us of who we are and where we've come from.

It provides a home and a community when we find life bleak and lonely.

And yet... the critics have a point.

The unpredictable flame of spirituality is often doused by the controlling hand of institutional religion.

And religion is only meaningful if it's informed by genuine spirituality. If it provides a home for authentic experience. If it opens a window into 'the other'.

True religion will always make room for a spirituality that will develop us, individually and collectively. A way to find ourselves. The American scholar Barbara Brown Taylor puts her finger on it: 'Religion is the deep well that connects me to the wisdom of the ages. Spirituality is the daily experience of hauling up living water and carrying it into a dry world.'[3]

As someone once said: 'Sitting in church on Sunday doesn't make you a Christian any more than standing in a garage makes you a car.'[4]

Morning has broken
Like the first morning,
Blackbird has spoken
Like the first bird.
Praise for the singing,
Praise for the morning,
Praise for them springing
fresh from the Word.

Sweet the rain's new fall.
Sunlit from heaven.
Like the first dewfall
on the first grass
Praise for the sweetness
of the wet garden
Sprung in completeness
where his feet pass

Mine is the sunlight,
Mine is the morning,
Born of the one light
Eden saw play;
Praise with elation,
Praise every morning,
God's recreation
Of the new day.[1]

Greet
the day

How many mornings will we get?

No one can tell.

The accident of birthplace has a say on the number of our days. But, roughly speaking, we might find the sun rising and peaking through our curtains about 26,000 times. We might lay down to rest 26,000 more.

At the end of it all, most of those days we will never remember. And a few we will never forget.

Nearly a century ago, the poet and children's author Eleanor Farjeon wrote the words to a hymn which beautifully captured a sense of gratitude for a new day. She imagined the first morning in Eden, with Adam and Eve taking in the birdsong, the dew on the grass, the breaking light. Much later the hymn became a hit for Cat Stevens, who continued to perform it under his new name, Yusuf Islam, after he converted to Islam.

Whether we give God a name or whether we don't, giving thanks is a good way to start the day.

What might happen on any given day? No one can tell. Every day is something of a surprise. All we can know for sure, as each new morning breaks, is that she is here again. She is ours.

'Give thanks for her,' says the cartoonist Michael Leunig, 'as you make your way.'[3]

This day before you now
Greet her with love and joy.
She is a fine strong person:
This precious living day
She is young and old
She is warm and cold
She is here for you
She will hold you well.
Make love with her
You'd be a fool to turn away
She is here. She is yours.
She is wise, she is hers.
She has dawned on you; this epic day.
Do not underestimate what she can do
Give thanks for her as you make your way.
Give thanks for the power and the kindness
Of this precious living day

Leunig

LIVE THE QUESTIONS

BE PATIENT TOWARD ALL THAT IS UNSOLVED IN YOUR HEART AND TRY TO LOVE THE QUESTIONS THEMSELVES, LIKE LOCKED ROOMS AND LIKE BOOKS THAT ARE NOW WRITTEN IN A VERY FOREIGN TONGUE. DO NOT NOW SEEK THE ANSWERS, WHICH CANNOT BE GIVEN YOU BECAUSE YOU WOULD NOT BE ABLE TO LIVE THEM. AND THE POINT IS, TO LIVE EVERYTHING. LIVE THE QUESTIONS NOW. PERHAPS YOU WILL THEN GRADUALLY, WITHOUT NOTICING IT, LIVE ALONG SOME DISTANT DAY INTO THE ANSWER.[1]

RAINER MARIA RILKE

Read the News

Are things getting better? Or worse?
Is history going forwards... or backwards?

Your answer may depend on anything from personality type to the headlines you woke up to on the morning news. Or, on who's asking the question. And where they're standing. But mostly your answer depends on what you mean by the question.
Do you mean: is the world a better place today than last year, or are things better in the twenty-first century than, say, in the nineteenth? Or in ancient times?

For example, in 1980, smallpox, which has existed for 3,000 years and was once one of the most feared diseases on the planet, was eradicated. The polio virus, which as recently as the 1980s, paralysed 350,000 people a year, is now almost gone too.

Or take life expectancy. If you're a woman in sub-Saharan Africa today, and you are asked if things are getting better and you compare yourself to the life of your grandmother, you may well say, 'yes'. Today, you will probably live until you are fifty-seven – that's sixteen years more of life than your grandmother, who might have made it to forty-one.

This kind of news doesn't make the headlines because it didn't happen an hour ago, or even yesterday. It didn't happen with the sickening thud of a bomb blast or the flash of a paparazzi camera. This is not twenty-four-hour rolling news but another sort that we rarely notice until, some time later – years, decades, centuries – someone decides to call it history.

Journalism is sometimes referred to as the first draft of history, but first drafts don't tell the whole story. In a world of 24/7 news, we can miss the bigger picture.

Each year, Bill Gates, one of the world's richest people, publishes a letter on behalf of his philanthropic foundation drawing on the latest research, from child mortality to economic growth. Recently Gates wrote:

'By almost any measure the world is better than it has ever been – by 2035 there will be almost no poor countries left in the world.'[1]

That sounds unlikely, but on the other hand, maybe Gates can see a more distant news cycle with a greater circumference.

Stand back a little, adjust your view and some days you might capture the faint outline of a more promising image of history.

Imagine it

Human beings are makers. We invent stuff: tools, machines, meals, stories, art, ideas, religions, cultures, mischief. Our capacity to create came in a 'cognitive revolution' around 70,000 years ago, according to the historian Yuval Noah Harari.[1] That's when Homo sapiens' capacity to create took off. And creation is one of the things that marks us out.

The engine of making is the imagination. And the fuel of that engine is a question. *What if?* A question that sends us way beyond straightforward invention.

What if I were you? In order for us to understand one another, we each need to imagine what it's like to *be* the other. Otherwise we do one another harm, trample over each others' feelings. To hurt someone else deliberately is a failure of the imagination. When we cry at weddings, view movies, watch our children play, we are imagining life through someone else's eyes.

Wouldn't it work better if? It takes imagination to plan anything: to develop a road system; to make a garden; to choose a school for our kids; to decide how much garlic to add to the casserole. To think ahead.

Couldn't we possibly? Crucially, our ability to hope is embedded in the imagination.

Anne Frank, Nelson Mandela, Rachel Carson, Harvey Milk and Malala Yousafzai envisioned a different, better world. Unless we can imagine that there is more than this, we're stuck in despair.

Is there more to life? Faith and belief are rarely built on certainties. They're based on imagination. For instance, thinking that there might be a God (or not), and trying to work out what that God might be like. That's why believers and doubters use metaphors for the divine: a parent, a despot, a shepherd, a friend. God is by definition *beyond* definition, so even in our understanding of the sacred, there's an element of invention.

What would happen if? Imagination opens us up to infinite possibilities, and leads to action.

Imagine it...

What would happen if you asked?

What would happen if you kissed him?

What would happen if you stopped it?

What would happen if you said goodbye?

What would happen if you... added some anchovy?

Ride your Luck

You've got to be in it to win it.

It *could* be you.

The chances are you'll play it this week. Or someone in your family will. Seventy per cent of people in the UK play the National Lottery regularly. They're betting that their number will come up. That luck will be on their side.

It's not logical. It's faith. Or maybe just fun.

The odds of winning the jackpot are 1 in 45 million. You are more likely to be crushed by a meteor (1 in 700,000), die from flesh-eating bacteria (1 in 1 million) or be hit by part of a plane falling from the sky (1 in 10 million).[1]

We can't prove luck exists but we often behave as if it does. 'Good luck,' we say, as if it will make some kind of difference. 'Bad luck!' we commiserate – as if some unseen force explains why your horse fell at the last, or you unexpectedly lost your job.

Why do we think it could be us? Perhaps it's evolutionary. Perhaps it's because the odds of just being alive on this good earth, in this strange universe, are so much longer.

Jim Al-Khalili, a theoretical physicist and former president of the British Humanist Association (now Humanists UK), writes:

'For me nothing makes life more worth living than the knowledge that my very existence is thanks to a colossal sequence of events since the beginning of the universe. Whether or not I was inevitable, how can I not be grateful for this privilege of being? And why would I not make the most of it?'[2]

Someone with a lot of time on their hands calculated the odds of any of us being born at one in ten... followed by two and three-quarter million zeroes. In other words, the odds of being alive are so improbable that winning the lottery looks quite plausible. Just by being here all our numbers came up.

And we're luckier still.

We can send our children to school, call on a doctor when we're sick, vote out politicians we don't like.

Most of this good fortune was made by people who came before us, people who got lucky with their own health or education, and decided to share their winnings by working for the rights we take for granted.

Religions find luck hard to explain. Faith and fate, divinity and destiny are not always good company. But whether we believe in God or don't, we lucked out just by being alive. Right here, right now.

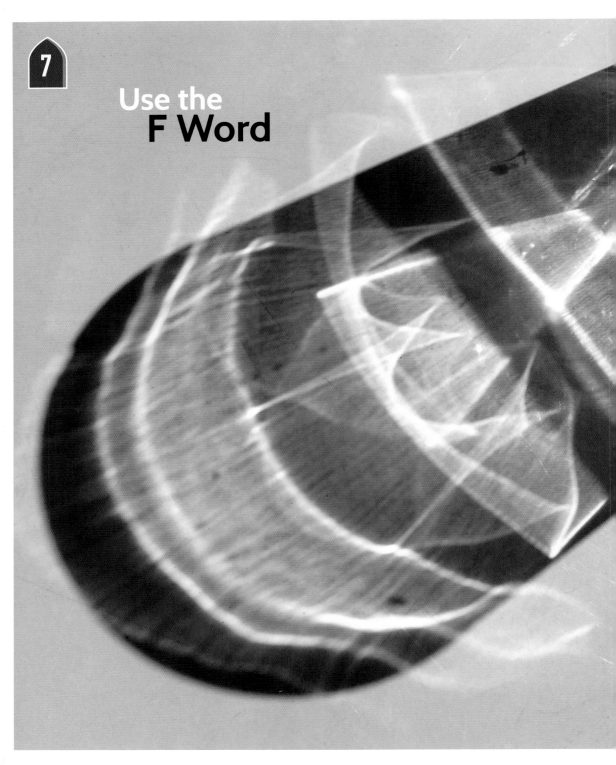

Use the
F Word

In March 1986, a gang armed with knives broke into a vicarage in Ealing, West London. During the assault Jill Saward, aged twenty-one, was raped; her boyfriend and father were beaten so violently that both were left with fractured skulls. But Jill's response was unexpected. 'I do not now, nor have I ever, hated the men who attacked me,' she said later. 'While I hated what they did to me, I was always able to distinguish between the act of aggression and the aggressors.'[1]

Jill Saward would dedicate the rest of her life to campaigning for the rights of survivors of sexual assault. As a Christian she was familiar with the words of the Lord's Prayer: 'Forgive us our sins as we forgive those who sin against us.' She said that there was never any question about forgiving her attackers, that was what her faith asked of her.

However, not everyone shares that faith. And not everyone who shares it, could make such a decision to forgive.

Forgiveness divides people. When the journalist Marina Cantacuzino, founder of the Forgiveness Project, was collecting stories of forgiveness and reconciliation for an exhibition called *The F Word*, she noticed that some people see forgiveness as a noble response to atrocity – and others see it as ridiculous. Even for those who believe in forgiveness, for most it will be a journey, not just in the face of the kind of brutal violation experienced by Jill Saward, but in the ordinary humdrum of our everyday relationships. Forgiveness is the WD-40 that smooths the creaking hinges of our relationships – and sometimes keeps the doors from falling off altogether.

'All friendships of any length,' says the poet David Whyte, 'are based on a continued, mutual forgiveness.'[2] Or as Martin Luther King Jr said: 'Forgiveness is not an occasional act, it is a constant attitude.'[3]

Touring with *The F Word* exhibition, highlighting people whose lives have been shattered by tragedy and violence, Marina Cantacuzino discovered that the process of being able to forgive has no set rules or time limits; it is not dependent on faith and it is often 'as mysterious as love'.[4]

She wanted to know if it can ease what George Eliot in *Middlemarch* called 'the hideous fettering of domestic hate'. It can, she concluded, but not in an instant. To forgive is both a choice and a process. 'I have come to see it as an intention,' writes Cantacuzino: 'a change of perspective, a direction to line yourself up for rather than a final and fixed destination. When it comes to considering forgiveness everyone has their limits, especially in the case of murder, genocide, rape, or violent extremism. However, within normal, everyday relationships forgiveness begins to feel more like a necessity than a choice.'[5]

And forgiveness does not always mean reconciliation. If someone is routinely abusing you, says Archbishop Desmond Tutu, you may be better off getting out of the relationship rather than seeking to fix it. Forgiveness brings reconciliation – if not with the person who has hurt you then with the lingering resentment they create.

The anger, bitterness, resentment and guilt that pursue violation can be potent. Hindsight will suggest alternative routes we might have taken and we may end up blaming ourselves, and also hating others. Sometimes the route to reconciliation is reconciliation with ourselves. This is succinctly expressed in a prayer of absolution found in the Prayer Book of the Anglican Church in New Zealand: 'God forgives you. Forgive others. Forgive yourself.'

Own up

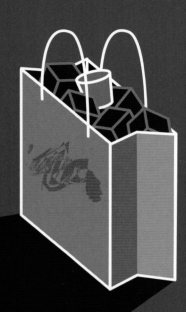

Self-service checkouts are turning us into a nation of shoplifters who steal almost £1.7 billion-worth of shopping a year: that was one newspaper's interpretation of a report into scan-it-yourself tills, which were 'just too tempting for one-in-five people, who admit they slip items they have not paid for into their bags'.[1]

Some people never seem to do anything wrong. It's always someone else's fault. Footballers seem especially good at this kind of body swerve. 'Never touched him, ref,' they maintain, all injured innocence. 'He dived!'

But it's all as old as the Garden of Eden. Take Adam and Eve and the Serpent. God catches Adam and accuses him of eating the forbidden fruit, he blames Eve, and then she blames the Serpent. Unfortunately, the Serpent, being limbless, had no fingers to point at someone else.

It's the universal story of temptation. We are just minding our own business, all innocent-like, when some devious inveigler catches us off guard and tricks us into doing the wrong thing. It wasn't me, it was them!

But is the self-service checkout possessed by a demon who makes us pocket the yoghurt? Is that what it means when it says 'unexpected item in the bagging area?' If we're offered a smartphone that's too cheap; if we're offered the chance to cheat on our partner; if cooking the books looks tempting – and we crumble, whose responsibility is it?

Mostly we create our own temptation. We wrestle with demons of our own making. We play the blame game only to find we're in a lose-lose situation.

If we're always looking for someone else to blame, we'll never consider owning up. Holding ourselves to account. And if we never face the music ourselves, we'll never take control of our lives.

Stay
Friends

Most of us have items of clothing that are old trusted friends. A thin T-shirt, washed soft and comfy; faded jeans that have shaped themselves to the contours of our body. They're part of the fabric of our existence.

Old friends share some of the same characteristics of old clothes. In the best sense, they're easy. Shared experiences and deep understanding means that an enormous amount can go unsaid. We settle into one another's company like an old armchair. One phrase, or the mention of someone's name, can set us off into uncontrolled laughter.

The poet Alden Nowlan[1] plumbs the depths of this kind of friendship in 'Great Things Have Happened':

We were talking about the great things
that have happened in our lifetimes;
and I said, 'Oh, I suppose the moon landing
was the greatest thing that has happened
in my time.' But, of course, we were all lying.
The truth is the moon landing didn't mean
one-tenth as much to me as one night in 1963
when we lived in a three-room flat...

... That night, the three of us, Claudine, Johnnie and me,
woke up at half-past four in the morning
and ate cinnamon toast together...

... it was like the feeling
you get sometimes in a country you've never visited
before, when the bread doesn't taste quite the same,
the butter is a small adventure, and they put
paprika on the table instead of pepper,
except that there was nobody in this country
except the three of us, half-tipsy with the wonder
of being alive, and wholly enveloped in love.

Close companionship fosters intimacy. And shared intimacy gives us permission to be honest with one another. It allows us both to support and challenge one another, because we're working from a position of mutual trust. There is no guile, no agenda. As the Hebrew proverb goes: 'Wounds from a friend can be trusted, while an enemy multiplies kisses.'

We need our friends like we need oxygen. The older our friendship, the more we need to acknowledge it, and them – especially when the shadows lengthen. Because that's when we need company. There's a verse that is said to come from the novelist Albert Camus or from a Jewish folk song; either way it rings true:

Don't walk in front of me; I may not follow.
Don't walk behind me; I may not lead.
Just walk beside me and be my friend.[2]

Helen Keller, the deaf-blind author and activist knew the value of this, saying, 'I would rather walk with a friend in the dark, than alone in the light.'[3] So did A. A. Milne's Piglet, in *The House at Pooh Corner*:[4]

Piglet sidled up to Pooh from behind.
'Pooh!' he whispered.
'Yes, Piglet?'
'Nothing,' said Piglet, taking Pooh's paw. 'I just wanted to be sure of you.'

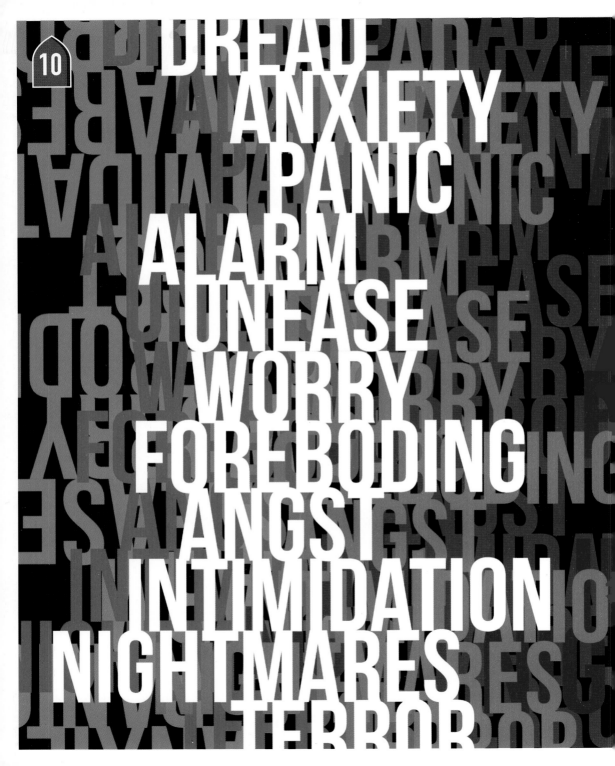

Fear Not.

Fear comes in all shapes and sizes. From whether you can get out of bed and face the day, to whether you can turn off the light and face the night. It's at the heart of what it means to be human:

The fear of the unknown or of the known.
The fear of not being in control.
The fear of missing out, the fear of taking part.
The fear of loving, the fear of not loving.
The fear of losing love.
The fear of not being good enough.
The fear of someone else – at work or on the street.
The fear of illness, the fear of death.
The fear of never having lived.

We all have fears, however secretly we harbour them. However much we deny them. Maybe it's some primal survival instinct, the suspicion that we're never quite safe and secure.

Although we may never be able to banish all our fears, we can make sure they don't banish us. We don't have to be managed by fear and insecurity. Of all the phrases in all the books in the Bible, the most common one goes like this: 'Have no fear.'

Or this: 'Do Not Be Afraid.'

Fear not. But how?

The Buddhist monk Thich Nhat Hanh says: 'The only way to ease our fear and be truly happy is to acknowledge our fear and look deeply at its source. Instead of trying to escape from our fear, we can invite it up to our awareness and look at it clearly and deeply.'[1]

Fear makes us defensive, turns us in on ourselves. It's opposite is not courage, but love. Love accepts, includes, is symbolised by open arms.

'There is no fear in love,' said the early Christian writer John, 'but perfect love casts out fear.'

> There are only two feelings.
>
> Love and fear.
>
> There are only two languages.
>
> Love and fear.
>
> There are only two activities.
>
> Love and fear.
>
> There are only two motives,
>
> two procedures, two frameworks,
>
> two results.
>
> Love and fear.
>
> Love and fear.[2]
>
> **MICHAEL LEUNIG**

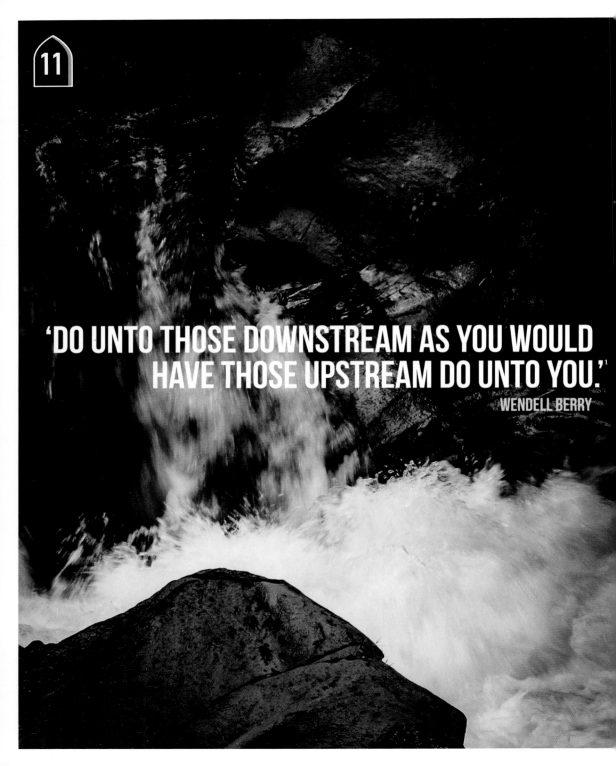

'DO UNTO THOSE DOWNSTREAM AS YOU WOULD HAVE THOSE UPSTREAM DO UNTO YOU.'[1]

WENDELL BERRY

It's often called the golden rule, and a version of it features in many of the great religious traditions.

In Islam it appears like this: 'No one of you is a believer until he desires for his brother that which he desires for himself.'

In Buddhism: 'Hurt not others in ways that you yourself would find hurtful.'

In Confucianism: 'Do not do to others what you do not want them to do to you.'

In Judaism: 'What is hateful to you, do not do to your fellow man. This is the law: all the rest is commentary.'

In Hinduism: 'This is the sum of duty: do not do to others what would cause pain if done to you.'

Someone summed it up as 'the Law of One':

'We are all one. When one is harmed, all are harmed. When one is helped, all are helped.' The ethic of reciprocity is the jargon term or, as Jesus of Nazareth put it: 'Do unto others as you'd have them do to you.'

While the idea is sanctified by religions, it's not owned by them. It's also cherished by people who don't buy religion at all. Putting yourself in someone else's shoes probably goes back before religion itself, before shoes too.

Empathy promotes kindness, compassion, understanding and respect. My decisions affect my neighbour – not just over the road but over the sea. On a neighbouring continent. Not just later today, but later in this century. Everyone's connected when we all share one planet.

Trust a farmer to understand. And a poet to capture it. That's Wendell Berry, who's both.

Stand still

Saint Kevin. Yes, there is one – the patron saint of people with mildly comic names like Malcolm, Mavis and Crispin.

St Kevin lived in Glendalough, County Wicklow in the sixth century. He was a hermit whose manmade cave was so small that when he prayed, with arms outstretched, he had to stick one of them out of the window.

One day, absorbed in prayerful contemplation, a blackbird landed on Kevin's hand. It was a long prayer and Kevin stood so still that the bird started to build a nest in the saint's upturned palm.

But now Kevin had a dilemma. Should he drop the nest or keep standing with his arm out? Well, being a saint, he decided to keep standing there, his arm stretched out like a branch. For weeks: while the blackbird laid her eggs; while she hatched them; while she fed her chicks; until the young fledged and flew the nest.

It's a tale celebrated by Seamus Heaney, who wrote that Kevin found himself 'linked into the network of eternal life'.[1] Heaney echoes the lines of William Blake in 'Auguries of Innocence' about holding 'infinity in the palm of your hand and eternity in an hour'.[2]

By becoming a kind of tree, Kevin was joined into the circle of life, death and rebirth. He was physically and metaphorically rooted, and by demonstrating his love for this bird and her brood, his body became a kind of living prayer sculpture.

Wildlife photographers – nature watchers of all kinds – talk about this quality of stillness, which enables them to disappear, and so to enable the life that is around them to be more fully itself. That standing still is an emptying, receptive process.

The Hebrew prophet Elijah, standing outside his cave, anticipated the voice of God in a thunderstorm or an earthquake or a fire. To his surprise, he found it in 'a sound of sheer silence'.

Pretending to be a tree for several weeks is a tough call, but the Spanish poet Pablo Neruda offers a more realistic practice. What if we stopped for one second, he asks, 'and not move our arms so much'. That would be 'an exotic moment'.[3]

To everything there is
a season

A mountain of courgettes. A heap of apples. A pile of peas. A hill of beans.

Summer and early autumn are ripe and luscious. In a good year – for even small-scale gardeners – there's too much to consume, which precipitates a flurry of freezing, pickling and preservation.

Yes, you can eat these all year round, plucked from supermarket shelves. But there's a delight in having to wait for the season to turn up, watching fruit and veg grow daily more plump and glossy, until that final moment when they're just right for table.

'To everything there is a season', says the ancient author of Ecclesiastes – whose ruminations were turned into a song, 'Turn! Turn! Turn!' by the folk singer Pete Seeger, and then made into a hit by the Byrds in 1965. There's 'a time to plant, a time to reap', Ecclesiastes goes. 'A time to weep, and a time to laugh; a time to mourn, and a time to dance.'

Harvest is a signal for feasting and festivity – born out of a year's laborious preparation: digging, tilling, feeding, waiting, weeding and protection.

Almost every celebration of any kind is all the sweeter when it comes out of a time of testing. A welcome pint after a hard week, or a decent lie-in after a run of broken nights. They're important tags, a way of saying anything from 'We did it!', to 'Phew, I'm glad that's over!'

Every year, Muslims mark Eid – an eruption of feasting that's been anticipated during the thirty days fasting of Ramadan. Jews think carefully about what delicacies they'll consume after the penitent fast of Yom Kippur. For Sikhs, the New Year festival of Baisakhi (or Vaisakhi) originally grew out of the harvest festivities in the Punjab. In the Christian calendar, the Easter festival emerges from the sombre forty days of Lent.

Life needs peaks to follow troughs: the first day of the school summer holidays; the clink of glasses that mark a birth; the fierce welcome hug at the airport arrivals gate; the first night's sleep back in your own bed.

Celebrations – whether they're religious or not – are holy moments. Holidays. They're like bookmarks telling us where we've got up to. They're an essential way of recognising that something significant has been achieved, of saying thank you to friends, family, teammates, the divine... whoever.

In a festive pause, we look one another in the eye, we repeat old stories, we raise a glass, we celebrate the past, and the present, and look to the future.

Write down
the day

We're all trying to get a better view of ourselves, but as there's so much of ourselves to see, perspective can be hard to come by. However, the simple act of setting pen to notepad and keeping a journal can help us step back and bring life into focus.

From the messiest scribble to the most considered and patient entry, a diary helps us stop, reflect and express who we are now. Taking time to write down our lives slows our racing thoughts, and briefly offers us the chance to see them in some kind of order. It enables us to get a feel for the shape of this life we're in. It helps us, says Joan Didion, 'remember what it was to be me. That is always the point.'[1]

In her book *The Artist's Way*, written to help people harness their innate creativity, Julia Cameron popularised the notion of producing 'Morning Pages' as a path to clear-headedness. Writing three pages, or 750 words, she recommends putting all your thoughts on the page for half an hour – including everything that's going wrong, the self-doubt, the criticism, the anxiety:

Once we get those muddy, maddening, confusing thoughts on the page, we face our day with clearer eyes. We are more honest with ourselves, more centred, and more spiritually at ease.[2]

Three pages may prove a luxury. On some mornings we seem to have no time; on others we seem to have nothing to say. But journal entries don't have to be long, deep or profound. They may be simple sketches or lists: music you're listening to; films you've seen; a novel that touched you. It might be as simple as a note of what someone said to you which you'd like to remember.

Other entries may dive down: asking yourself why a relationship has gone pear-shaped; musing on whether you really could leave your job and change career. Even entries which seem like a dump of inarticulate feelings can, later, glint with moments of clarity.

To distinguish a diary from the week's routine writing, it can help to write by hand, not on screen, to set aside a book which you don't use for anything else – and to keep it private. You can be much more honest with yourself if you know no one else is going to read what you write.

A diary may only be cursory, a snapshot. But over time it can become an increasingly reliable witness to your life. As you re-read entries from months or years before, sometimes a journal can become a map of your days, warning you about blind alleys and cul-de-sacs, and, in hilly terrain, encouraging you with a reminder of the view ahead.

Step out of the routine of daily obligations. Step back from the minutiae of each day. Take a look at your life in the round. Record your days. Listen back. See who you are.

start here

keep going >

LISTEN TO YOUR LIFE

SEE IT FOR THE FATHOMLESS MYSTERY IT IS. IN THE BOREDOM AND PAIN OF IT NO LESS THAN IN THE EXCITEMENT AND GLADNESS: TOUCH, TASTE, SMELL YOUR WAY TO THE HOLY AND HIDDEN HEART OF IT BECAUSE IN THE LAST ANALYSIS ALL MOMENTS ARE KEY MOMENTS, AND LIFE ITSELF IS GRACE.[1]

FREDERICK BUECHNER, NOVELIST

Be kind

Proverbs are back. Short, pithy sayings which make you laugh, surprise you with a twist, or invite you to think twice about your day. Authorship is often contested. As Abraham Lincoln himself once put it: 'The trouble with quotes on the internet is that you never know if they're genuine.'

Among the millions of online aphorisms, few have gained popularity and staying power like the following soundbite by the ancient Greek philosopher Plato. 'Be kind, for everyone you meet is fighting a hard battle.'

Actually, as Lincoln would have undoubtedly pointed out (had he not died 150 years before the arrival of the internet), Plato did not say this, but the attribution doubtless contributes to its longevity. It was probably coined by the nineteenth-century Scottish writer Ian McClaren who, when asked by a religious weekly for a Christmas message, replied: 'Be pitiful, for every man is fighting a hard battle.'

We wouldn't use the word 'pity' these days, we might use the word 'empathy', a quality that we cannot underestimate according to anthropologist Jane Goodall:

Empathy is really important. Only when our clever brain and our human heart work together in harmony can we achieve our true potential.[1]

In public or in private, all of us are wrestling with the complexities of living this life – from how to negotiate a relationship to how to pay the bills. Some days are difficult and resolution refuses to arrive. Responding with kindness will never make things worse – and usually make them better.

'Kindness is like water,' says the Dalai Lama, 'religion like tea.'[2]

Come again?

In *Ethics are More Important than Religion* he describes how the tea we drink is made mostly of water, but it also contains other ingredients as well to make it taste good. But however we make it, the main ingredient of tea is always water. And when push comes to shove, we can live without tea, but not without water. Likewise, he says, 'we are born without religion, but not without the basic need for compassion'.

In other words, while the human race could probably survive without religion, we don't stand a chance without kindness.

Trade stories

Our lives are shaped by stories. They're stories in themselves. When we meet someone new we begin by telling them our story: where we come from, who our parents were, where we went to school... what happened on the next page, the next chapter. We're all storytellers.

Our nations and tribes, our faith traditions and families are built on stories. Defining myths, victories, defeats, parables, folktales, anecdotes – history, herstory.

Some of the tales we tell are rooted in actuality, others are embroidered. Some are made up from scratch. But – fact, fiction or faction – they're often 'true'. Before modernity and fundamentalism burdened us with an obsession with fact and literalism, people would seldom ask of a story: 'Did it happen?' Instead they'd ask: 'Is it true?' They sensed that, in the words of poet Mary Oliver, 'they won't be false, and they won't be true but they'll be real'.[1]

Flannery O'Connor put it perfectly: 'I'm always highly irritated,' she said, 'by people who imply that writing fiction is an escape from reality – it's a plunge *into* reality.'[2]

That's why humankind has always told tales. 'After nourishment, shelter and companionship, stories are the thing we need most in the world,' says Philip Pullman.[3] Stories are how we articulate our values, longings and anxieties – how we pass on what's important to our children. 'Stories show us how to bear the unbearable, approach the unapproachable, conceive the inconceivable,' says writer Melanie Tem. 'Stories provide meaning, texture, layers and layers of truth.'[4]

Stories give us room to grow. C. S. Lewis, whose *The Lion, the Witch and the Wardrobe* continues to capture the imaginations of new generations of children, put it like this:

We seek an enlargement of our being. We want to be more than ourselves. Each of us by nature sees the whole world from one point of view with a perspective and a selectiveness peculiar to ourselves... we want to see with other eyes, to imagine with other imaginations, to feel with other hearts, as well as with our own... We demand windows... my own eyes are not enough for me. I will see through the eyes of others.[5]

Sharing our own lived experiences, trading stories with one another, is a way of revealing that there are new possibilities, alternative narratives. Another way to travel, as Jeanette Winterson says: 'True stories are the ones that lie open at the border, allowing a crossing, a further frontier...'[6]

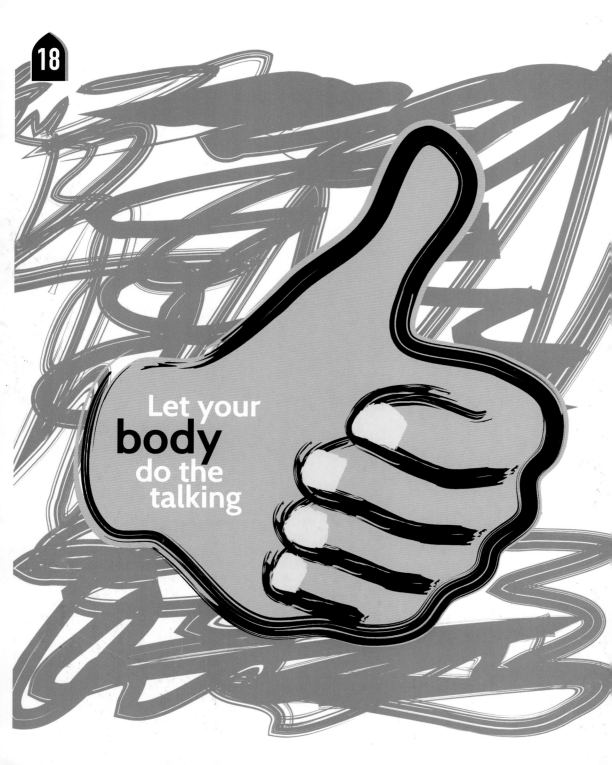

Let your
body
do the
talking

'If it's something you understand,' said the fourth-century Christian teacher Augustine, 'then it's not God.'[1]

Still, throughout history, we've tried to understand God and then tried to capture the understanding in language. Usually in words.

In the Christian tradition people came up with creeds – formulaic collections of dogmatic statements designed to button down correct belief. And they sought to exclude what they thought was incorrect, which came to be known as heresy. It took ages. For example, the most widely agreed creed used in churches today wasn't settled on until around 300 years after Jesus's death. It's framed like a legal contract. (Sign here.):

... the only Son of God,
eternally begotten of the Father,
before all worlds,
God from God, Light from Light,
true God from true God,
begotten, not made,
being of one Being with the Father.[2]

It's unlikely Jesus's friends in first-century Palestine would have addressed him using language like this, unless they were taking the rise out of his growing reputation. Most of the time he was a bit of an enigma – often quite shy about revealing himself. There were times when he even told witnesses not to let on about some remarkable act he'd been involved in.

Whatever his friends thought about him, Jesus often gave the impression he felt called to speak for God. What we know about his life suggests he was onto something that we all should know. The novelist Tim Winton puts it like this: 'Christ is an imaginative avenue to a larger mystery, the Divine.'[3]

Those who choose to follow the life of compassion, healing and generosity Jesus modelled think it signals something unique. Not just what he said, but who he was. 'A body language for God,'[4] is how the theologian Mark Oakley phrases it. A body language of signs and signals, an imaginative way of communication which is less precise and more open than words. Maybe that's why one of the earliest records of Jesus's life says that he spoke in parables all the time: 'Without a parable he told them nothing.'[5]

These stories were open to interpretation, meaning different things to different people. Pretty much like Jesus's life itself, says Professor Nicola Slee: 'It is a story characterised by elements of shock, surprise, extravagance and reversal, and like the parables it is a story that is open to multiple interpretation, thus respecting both the freedom and creative imagination of every reader.'[6]

Who we are, and how we live, may be more significant than what we believe or how we say it. As Francis of Assisi is reputed to have told his followers: 'Preach the good news at all times and, if necessary, use words.'

Seize the day

Some days you wake up and it feels like morning hasn't come. And that it won't. You reach for the alarm and turn it off and now the alarm's inside you. Warning you this will be a dark day. And then that thing which is not light dawns on you.

She's gone.

He's not going to make it.

It's over.

Perhaps it's less personal, more political. It really happened. Change was going to come, and it came, and it was not a good change.

The sense of dread rises. Queasiness. The pit in your stomach as your fears become physical.

Notice these emotions, don't deny them, says the Persian poet Rumi:[1] 'Even if they're a crowd of sorrows who violently sweep your house empty of its furniture.'

These sorrows don't have to be buried. Bleak is how some days look, and we don't have to know how to react. We might have to sit in this gloom for a while. Perhaps time will help our sight adjust.

'Dear Americans,' wrote Canadian novelist Margaret Atwood, the day after the 2016 US presidential election: 'It will be all right in the long run. (How long? We will see.) You've been through worse, remember.'[2]

'History takes such a long, long time,' as the songwriter Bruce Cockburn,[3] sang. It was our mistake to think we could dictate its arrival time. No one knew this better than Civil Rights activist Martin Luther King, even on the darkest days. 'The arc of the moral universe is long,' he insisted, 'but it bends towards justice.'[4]

Hope is not a synonym for optimism. Optimism is generated by the available evidence. But hope, says Professor Cornel West, will dare to defy the evidence. Hope says we can 'go beyond the evidence to create new possibilities... to allow people to engage in heroic actions always against the odds, no guarantee whatsoever'.[5]

No guarantee, but our agnosticism about the future provides what essayist Rebecca Solnit calls a 'spaciousness of uncertainty'. 'Hope,' she says 'is a sense of the grand mystery of it all, the knowledge that we don't know how it will turn out, that anything is possible.'[6]

The waiting is our chance to decide how we'd like things to be. 'Hope imagines the future,' says theologian Walter Wink. 'And then acts as if that future is irresistible.'[7] People of faith may draw on the conviction that good is at work in history, the hope the ancient psalmist had when she could say: 'Even though I walk through the darkest valley, I will fear no evil, for you are with me; your rod and your staff, they comfort me.'[8]

For others, hope may rest in a sense that, for all the wrong turns, history's general direction of travel is promising. The novelist E. B. White put this beautifully in a letter to a reader who harboured doubts about the future of humanity. Human society, wrote White, reminded him of how sailors talk

of the weather as 'a great bluffer': 'Things can look dark, then a break shows in the clouds, and all is changed, sometimes rather suddenly... Hang on to your hat. Hang on to your hope. And wind the clock, for tomorrow is another day.'[9]

The break in the clouds may come to us as friend, or stranger. As unexpected event. Even unwelcome. J. R. R. Tolkien, who had seen darker days than most in the trenches of the First World War, refused to give up on hope. Perhaps this was at the back of his mind when he wrote a scene in *The Lord of the Rings*, as war approached in Middle Earth:

'"I wish it need not have happened in my time," said Frodo.

"So do I," said Gandalf, "And so do all who live to see such times. But that is not for them to decide. All we have to decide is what to do with the time that is given to us."'[10]

Trust your instinct

On the first day in a new job, or at a new school, your antennae go into overload. Particularly when it comes to the people with whom you'll be sharing this habitat. Every receptor you have is on alert for signals. Is she snooty or just shy? Is he genuinely friendly, or over-compensating? Why does she do that thing with her hair? Does he always sit like that? Do I like her? Can I trust him?

'It would be interesting,' says the essayist Malcolm Gladwell in his book *Blink*, 'to find out what goes on in that moment when someone looks at you and draws all sorts of conclusions.'[1] No one single sense is involved in these perceptions: it's all of them, at the same time. We get a reading off someone in an instant. Call it gut feeling, instinct, intuition, hunch.

These readings, which we receive from people, places or situations, aren't logical constructions. They don't come from reasoning; they tend to arrive as a hit. But that doesn't mean we can't trust them. Often our instinctive decryptions are a mash up of lived experience, emotion, body language and more.

Yes, sometimes our own bad past experiences can make us fearful, or defensive, and give us false readings. And other people's insecurities can mean they jam their own signals. So, it's not always wise to rush to judgement. Nonetheless, our instincts are pretty reliable. And in the normal round of life, work and relationships, we can't give one another

the kind of vetting necessary for joining the security services. The singer Bono puts it like this: 'I've always believed in instinct over intellect. The instinct is what you always knew; intellect is what you figure out.'[2]

We take a leap of faith and, Gladwell says, 'There can be as much value in the blink of an eye as in months of rational analysis.'[3]

We need to be able to put our trust in our instincts and in each other, even if it's provisional. The broadcaster Melvyn Bragg believes that faith and instinct are kissing cousins: 'I think faith is the great undiscovered region of our minds. It's like instinct, which I've always thought is compressed intelligence, at such a high speed you can't see it, as fast as a blink.'[4]

Like instinct, he says, 'faith is very often a whole perception which has to be (as it were) deconstructed into what is plausible and what is not'.[5]

We can lean on our instinct, faith – lay bets on it. We have to, otherwise we can't make relationships. But we also need to interrogate it. Left unquestioned, instinct can become bigotry, phobia. But when our instincts warm us to people, to ideas, and ways of living, life unfurls. In the words of Ralph Waldo Emerson:

All our progress is an unfolding, like a vegetable bud. You have first an instinct, then an opinion, then a knowledge as the plant has root, bud, and fruit. Trust the instinct to the end, though you can render no reason.[6]

Tune in

George Herbert, the seventeenth-century metaphysical poet, wrote a poem about prayer, 'Prayer (I)', without explaining what prayer was. Just as well. 'Hands together, heads bowed, eyes closed' doesn't really do it.

But he hinted at what can happen when people try to pray. And his best hint was simply this: 'something understood'.

Every now and again. For a second – or less – we luck out on an 'aha!' moment. Something understood… even if it remains something we can't quite explain.

Most faiths involve prayer and while some, like Buddhism, don't rely on a god, the emerging discipline of 'mindfulness' offers a way of 'prayer' that doesn't rely on faith. Prayer is tuning in. Opening ourselves to hearing 'the tune which all things hear' as Herbert phrases it. It's about joining a conversation with whatever or whoever may be within, behind or beyond it all. It's about another way of being. Herbert calls it: 'The soul in paraphrase.'[1]

You can kneel, sit in the lotus position, prostrate yourself, go for a stroll.

You can breathe, chant, mutter, shout, say nothing.

You can flatter, beg, reason, provide a shopping list, empty yourself.

You can use a prayer book, repeat a mantra, make it up as you go along, live it out.

You can address God, speak to the trees, petition the dead, talk to yourself.

You can pray deliberately or allow it to happen.

You can be by yourself, or with others.

'It doesn't matter how you pray,' says novelist Anne Lamott: 'With your head bowed in silence, or crying out in grief, or dancing. Churches are good for prayer, but so are garages and cars and mountains and showers and dance floors… Some people think that God is in the details, but I have come to believe that God is in the bathroom.'[2]

Prayer is not about cause and effect. Or at least not in any way that anyone has ever convincingly explained. Prayer is about changing ourselves, and so changing the world. There is only one rule in prayer: the rule of waiting. Ann Lewin, in her poem 'Disclosure'[3], says that it's like waiting to catch sight of a kingfisher:

All you can do is
Be where he is likely to appear, and
Wait.

And yet, she says, 'Often, nothing much happens':

There is space, silence and
Expectancy.
No visible sign, only the
Knowledge that he's been there
And may come again.

But sometimes, when you've almost stopped expecting anything,

…a flash of brightness
Gives encouragement.

Make a
habit of it

It's Sunday morning, and some ancient programming hardwired deep inside tells someone to go to church.

Perhaps it would be a big decision if they decided *not* to do it, but in recent decades millions of people have made that very decision. They have reprogrammed themselves: they enjoy a divine lie-in on Sunday morning; they drink coffee and read the paper, catch up on Facebook, call relatives, go to the supermarket, hang out.

In the UK the numbers participating in institutional religion are falling, steadily. It's the default position. No religion is the new religion.

But still, around the world, a lot of people continue to wear the religious habit. In Kampala and Manila, in Buenos Aires and Bethlehem, in Ho Chi Minh City and in Holloway, north London... on Sundays, people do church.

On Friday, Muslims say prayers at the mosque.

On Saturday, Jews walk to synagogue.

It's a ritual. It's a habit.

Taken together, our habits shape the lives we live. And good habits are a good habit. When life gets tough, they can help us find hope. 'Hope begins in the dark,' writes Anne Lamott. 'The stubborn hope that if you just show up and try to do the right thing, the dawn will come.'[1]

U. A. Fanthorpe in her poem 'Atlas', shows how the ordinary, overlooked habits of the everyday can become a beautifully engineered pattern, strong enough to hold up an entire life:

There is a kind of love called maintenance
Which stores the WD40 and knows when
to use it.[2]

She goes on to talk about how this hands-on, daily detail, love – leaves notes for the milkman; answers letters; makes dental appointments; reviews the car insurance. Like Atlas, she says, this 'upholds/The permanently rickety elaborate/Structures of living...'

Any healthy life needs good habits. Although in religion, habit is often called ritual. Like our other daily habits – cleaning our teeth in the bathroom each morning – once we're in the place of worship, the programming takes over.

Christians, for example, sing songs, make a confession, receive bread and wine, say prayers, give money away, listen to a talk, wonder what it's about, hope it will soon be over. Many of them have undergone rituals called baptism, or confirmation – public commitments that they will try and follow the way of Jesus of Nazareth.

The scholar Karen Armstrong writes:

'Religion is not about accepting 20 impossible propositions before breakfast, but about doing things that change you. It is a moral aesthetic, an ethical alchemy. If you behave in a certain way, you will be transformed.'[3]

Like other habits, we choose some rituals after deliberation, and some we do automatically, without thinking. But all of them contribute to the kind of people we want to be. Our habits inform how we live, without us realising it.

Rituals can be a performance that needs no explaining. Like a mantra, the repetition itself is the meaning. 'Ritual is poetry in action,' said Rabbi Chaim Stern.[4]

The best kind of rituals are a really good habit. 'We are what we repeatedly do,' Aristotle put it a millennia and a half ago. 'Excellence is not an act, but a habit.'[5]

TELL IT LIKE IT IS

Most of us are happy giving organisations and institutions a piece of our mind. It's a vital part of our liberty to call such monoliths and their ethos to account. As writer Salman Rushdie says: 'The moment you say that any idea system is sacred, whether it's a religious belief system or a secular ideology, the moment you declare a set of ideas to be immune from criticism, satire, derision, or contempt, freedom of thought becomes impossible.'[1]

But what about when it gets personal? What do we do when someone we know needs to be brought to book? How honest are we prepared to be?

'Criticism may not be agreeable, but it is necessary,' said Winston Churchill. 'It fulfils the same function as pain in the human body; it calls attention to the development of an unhealthy state of things.'[2] Constructive criticism – from a coach, a mentor or a tutor – is essential for anyone who wants to improve their performance, in whatever field. And we're sometimes too close to see what we're doing wrong, or how to correct it.

If someone's actions are in danger of ruining their own lives, or hurting other people, then we have a duty to intervene. It's the shadow side of kindness. Another world leader from another century, Abraham Lincoln, said: 'He has a right to criticise, who has a heart to help.' But it's then a question of how, and when.

The playwright Alan Bennett once said that there's only one appropriate response on an opening night, and that's: 'Marvelous, marvellous, marvellous!'[3] Anything else appears niggardly, cruel and discouraging to someone who's at their most vulnerable. But what about that creaky bit in the second act? To be fair, Bennett isn't saying that we ignore defects, it's a matter of waiting until the excitement and paranoia has died down.

When one of Lincoln's generals, say, screwed up, he would write him an enraged letter pointing out his deficiencies in excoriating detail. He called these his 'hot' letters. But they would remain unposted. He would put them in an envelope, marked, 'never sent, never signed'. He waited for his rage to cool before delivering a more measured critique.

We live in the age of the 'hot' email, when we unload our vitriol on unsuspecting victims. This purging may be of some temporary use to us but not to anyone else. If we want to help someone else effect change, then we need to couch honest criticism in a positive framework.

In management speak, there's a (much-derided) feedback technique known as the 'shit sandwich'. You start by telling your colleague how well they're generally doing, before forensically pulling apart their performance. You then end by saying how much better it's going to be from now on. Critics of this critique have a point. It's a formula which doesn't recognise that individuals respond to criticism – and how it's delivered – very differently. Some will only hear the good news; some will only hear the bad.

We have to gauge our honesty, and our criticism, to each circumstance and individual. But the shit still needs some kind of positive, helpful sandwich, otherwise it's simply belittling. The only point of honest criticism is to help us get better. That's why we need critical friends. As the tender, ancient psalmist pleaded: 'Smite me in kindness.'

24

Be more
Beastly

We're animals.

Most of us recognise this. We share a great deal with our fellow creatures. But how much?

The jury is still out on whether we humans are simply top of the animal class, or if we're in a class of our own.

The origins of humankind are a mystery – not something we can be entirely certain about. The model that most people who study these things suggest is that Homo sapiens first emerged between 250,000 and 400,000 years ago. It seems that for a while we hung around, developed some basic tools, but didn't exactly set the world alight, even if we had discovered how to light a fire.

Having migrated from Africa into Europe and managed, somehow, to elbow the Neanderthals out of the way, we seem – roughly 30–70,000 years ago – to have gone through some kind of cognitive revolution, what the historian Yuval Noah Harari calls 'the Tree of Knowledge mutation'[1]. We developed new ways of thinking and communicating. Our language became more complex and nuanced, our ability to cooperate and organise together was enhanced. We invented boats, oil lamps, bows and arrows, needles. And significantly, we developed art, religion, cultures.

We think, we organise, we create. We wonder what happens to us when we die. If we're not careful, this facility can give us a kind of self-conscious swagger. And then it's worth recalling that, a couple of million years before, we were emerging from a genus of apes called Australopithecus.

We're still animals at heart.

Sometimes, when we're inclined to over-engineer our lives and our surroundings, when we're overwrought with anxiety we'd do well to recall those origins. Wendell Berry, the Kentucky farmer, poet and essayist takes refuge in the animal world in his poem 'The Peace of Wild Things':[2]

*When despair for the world grows in me
and I wake in the night at the least sound
in fear of what my life and my children's lives
may be,
I go and lie down where the wood drake
rests in his beauty on the water, and the great
heron feeds.
I come into the peace of wild things
who do not tax their lives with forethought
of grief. I come into the presence of still water.
And I feel above me the day-blind stars
waiting with their light. For a time
I rest in the grace of the world, and am free.*

The relative simplicity, the elemental nature of animal life, also has profound messages for those of us who tend to embellish what is essentially an intuitive longing to search for what might be beyond ourselves with elaborate structures of observance and protocol. Walt Whitman says it like this:

*[Animals] do not sweat and whine about their condition,
They do not lie awake in the dark and weep for their sins,
They do not make me sick discussing their duty to God.
Not one is dissatisfied, not one is demented
with the mania of owning things...*[3]

Maybe we're just trying too hard, and should relax. Be a bit more beastly.

25

Pursue
kindness

In a crowded train carriage, Sammy Welch was entertaining her young son Rylan on the five-hour journey from Birmingham, in the middle of England, to Plymouth, on the southwest coast.

Someone noticed what a good job she was doing in trying circumstances and after a stop in Wiltshire, Sammy found a note left on the table. 'Have a drink on me,' it read. 'You're a credit to your generation, polite and teaching the little boy good manners.' It was signed: 'Man on the train at table with glasses and hat.' There was a five-pound note with it.

Ms Welch was overwhelmed by the stranger's generosity: 'There are good people out there,' she said. 'I want him to know I'm truly grateful.'[1]

Unexpected generosity like this is often billed as a 'random act of kindness'. The phrase is traced back to a note left in a San Francisco restaurant thirty years ago by the writer Anne Herbert.

'Practice random kindness,' she wrote, 'and senseless acts of beauty.' She wrote a book documenting true stories of acts of kindness and the idea took off, morphing into a cultural meme informing TV shows, websites and films like *Evan Almighty* – in which God tells the hero Evan to change the world with one act of random kindness at a time.

But what if God was wrong? Why leave kindness to chance? Why not make kindness deliberate, planned and organised?

What family settles for random parenting? ('I know she's only three, darling but I thought she might like to drive the car.') An employee who only turns up to work when they feel like it would soon be an ex-employee. We're generally suspicious of politicians making up quick-fix policy on the hoof and prefer those with a considered plan.

The same goes for kindness: random is fine, but routine is divine. Kindness is at the heart of a good life.

'My religion is very simple,' says the Dalai Lama. 'My religion is kindness.'[2]

The world, runs a luminous phrase buried in the Book of Psalms, 'is built of kindness'. When you get dressed, said the early Christian writer Paul, 'clothe yourselves with kindness'.

Kindness, said the Prophet Muhammad, 'is a mark of faith, whoever is not [kind]; has no faith'.

This is less about spontaneous acts ignited by feelings of compassion or indignation, and more a decision to follow a way of life signposted by mercy, generosity and justice. It's less about a breaking emotional wave and more about a steady, reliable tide of good action.

The Ancient Greek Aesop was right: 'No act of kindness, no matter how small, is ever wasted.'

Random kindnesses, like an anonymous note to a loving mum on a train, can be wonderful. But regular, repeated and routine kindness will transform life even more deeply.

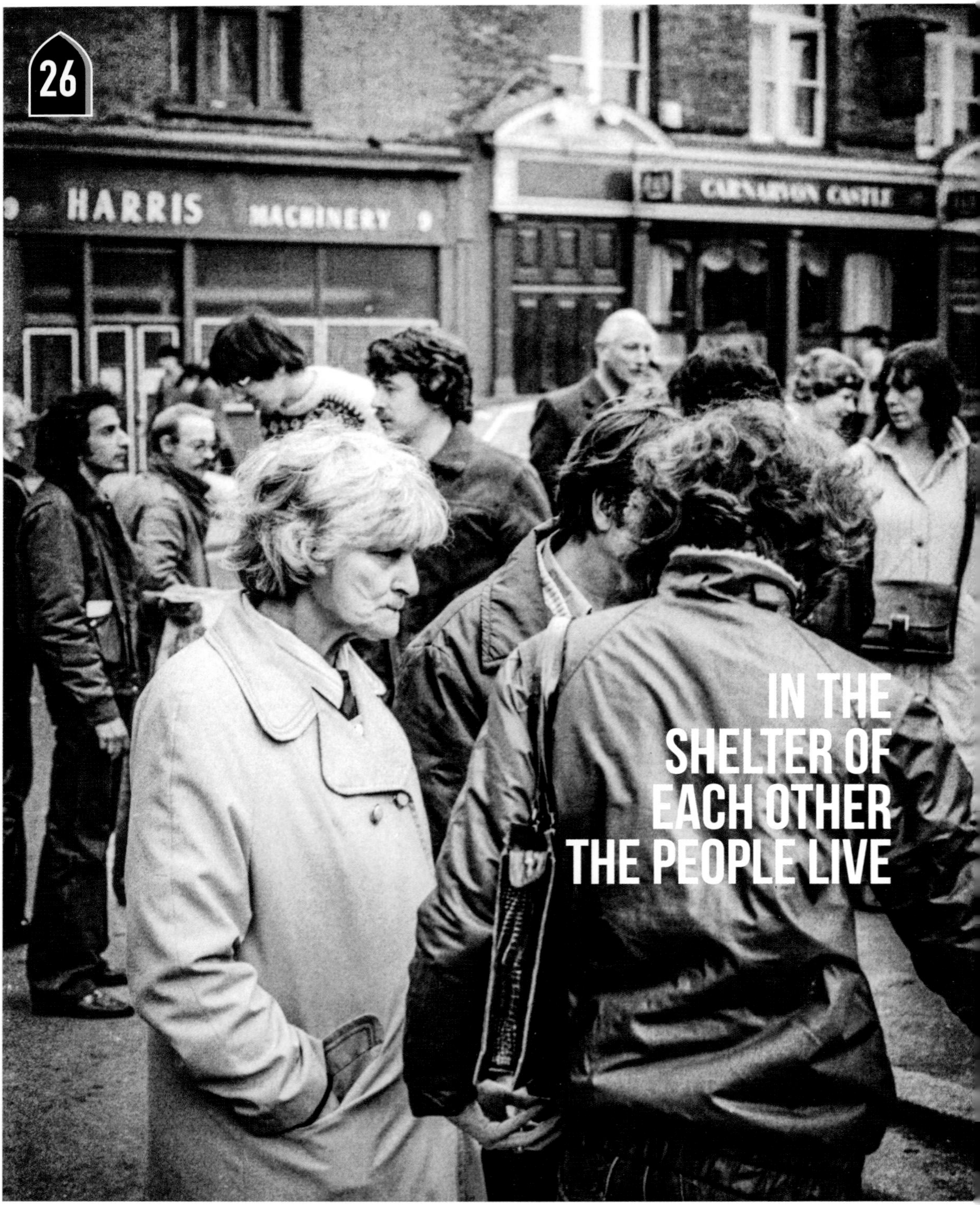

26

IN THE
SHELTER OF
EACH OTHER
THE PEOPLE LIVE

In the name of goodness, of love and of broken community
in the name of meaning, of feeling and I hope you don't screw me
in the name of darkness and light and ungraspable twilight
in the name of mealtimes and sharing and caring by firelight

In the name of action, of peace and of human redemption
in the name of eating, of drinking and table confession
in the name of sadness, regret and holy obsession
in the holy name of anger, the spirit of aggression

In the name of forgive and forget, and I hope I get over this
in the name of fathers and mothers and unholy spirits
in the name of beauty and broken and beaten up daily
in the name of seeing our creeds and believing in maybe

We gather here, a roomful of strangers
and speak of our hopeland, and talk of our danger
to make sense of our thinking, to authenticate lives
to humanise feeling and stop telling lies

In the name of philosophy, of theology and who gives a damn
in the name of employment and study and finding new family
in the name of our passions, our lovings and indecent obsessions
in the name of prayer, of worship and demon possession

In the name of solitude, of quiet and holy reflection
in the name of the lost, the lonely and the without-direction
in the name of the early and the late and the wholly ineffectual
in the name of the straight and the queer, transgender and bisexual

In the name of bootclogs, and boobjobs and erectile dysfunction,
in the name of schizophrenia, hysteria and obsessive compulsion
in the name of Jesus, and Mary and the mostly silent Joseph
in the name of speaking to ourselves saying 'this is more than I can cope with'

In the name of touchup, and breakup, and of breakdown-and-weeping
in the name of therapy, and Prozac, and of full-hearted breathing
in the name of sadness and madness and years-since-I've- smiled
in the name of the Unknown, the Alien, and of the Wholly-in-Exile

In the name of the named and the unnamed and the names of the nameless
In the name of the prayers that repeat 'I wish that I could change this'
In the name of goodness and kindness and intentionality
In the name of harbour, and shelter and family

'IN THE NAME'[1], *by the Irish poet and theologian* **Pádraig Ó Tuama**, *resonates with a saying in Irish:* Ar scáth a cheile a mhaireas na daoine. *Rendered in English, it reads: 'It is in the shelter of each other that the people live.'*

27

Improve your image

Images, said Pope Gregory the Great, are for the ignorant. But his holiness wasn't being as ignorant as he sounds. In AD 600, one of his bishops had been destroying religious art in churches, alarmed in case people should treat them as idols. Gregory told him to stop. Religious images were useful: 'What scripture is to the educated, images are to the ignorant.' Images were a way of teaching 'truth' to those who couldn't read.

This was something of a backhanded compliment to the visual arts, inferring that words were the superior medium, and images merely a substitute. But Gregory spoke against a backdrop of long-standing suspicion of certain kinds of visual image in Judaism, Christianity and Islam. In Judaism there is a prohibition in depicting Yahweh, while Muslims are forbidden to depict Allah and Muhammed. Christianity has hosted a constant battle for supremacy between word and image.

All these prohibitions sprang from a fear by the religious thought police that making pictures or sculptures of the divine or her prophets would reduce them to the human plane. Or encourage idolatory – people worshipping the pictures. Worse still, visual images were dangerous, because it's difficult to pin down their precise meaning. Words have definitions. With words you can form doctrines, creeds, codes, propositions. You can tell people what they are to believe. You can point to the written authority.

But an image is looser, more open-ended. It provides emotional and aesthetic wiggle room. People can populate images with their own feelings and meanings. They can take them away, and make them personal.

This isn't to say that images don't have their own language. There's a non-verbal vocabulary of signs and symbols which to those able to read them can enrich art's meaning. But it isn't essential to be able to 'read' a painting or sculpture to be nourished by it. Images reach parts of us that words can't.

Regardless of whether an image is figurative, abstract, religious, secular, it's possible for something unspoken to pass between the artist and the viewer. The visual is a medium purpose built for the indefinable, the mysterious.

The blurred blue–grey in a Rothko can make you shiver.

A Frida Kahlo can make you question yourself.

A Georgia O'Keeffe flower can stir your senses.

A lived-in Rembrandt face can bring you to your knees.

'If I can't picture it,' said Albert Einstein, 'I can't understand it.'

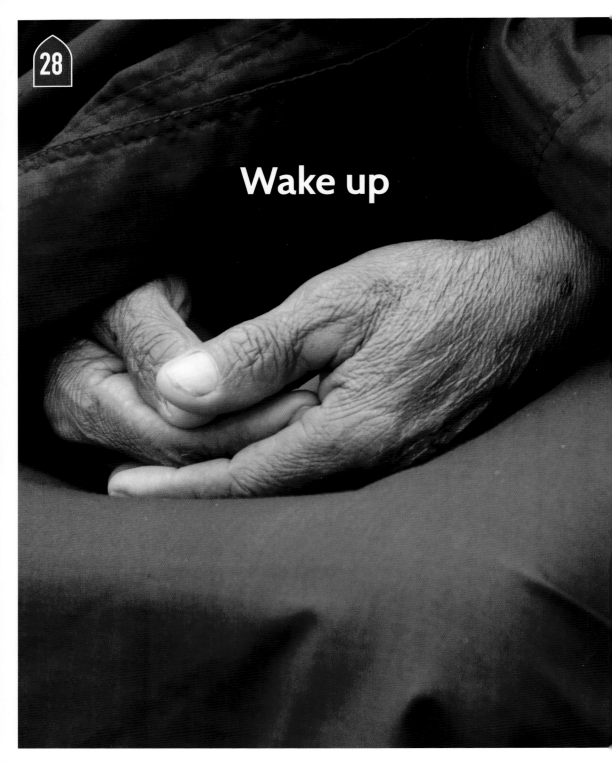

28

Wake up

Why do we pray? We do it because we're human. We've always done it.

Five thousand years ago people sacrificed animals to secure divine protection; today we might give thanks over an animal we're about to eat. Prayer evolves. From spoken word to physical signs: we bow our heads and close our eyes, we kneel, we invite children to put their hands together.

At Jerusalem's Western Wall, devout Jews sway back and forth as they pray. Sufi Muslims whirl around, looking for the sweet spot of divine connection. Hindus chant. Quakers maintain silence, hoping to tune in to a divine frequency. A Muslim will stop five times a day, turn East to face Mecca, kneel and pray. Buddhists breathe...

Christians pray because, like Islam, their story springs from the Hebrew tradition, one which opens in a garden where God is talking with Eve and Adam. The first prayer. This is a tradition which features an entire anthology of sung prayers, the Book of Psalms, a collection of people arguing with God, begging God, longing for God, praising God, politely requesting God. People who take it as read that connecting with the divine is how to live the good life.

'On my bed I remember you,' says one psalmist, 'I think of you through the watches of the night. Because you are my help, I sing in the shadow of your wings. My soul clings to you; your right hand upholds me.'[1]

Christian story emerges, prayer is just as essential to a good life, but even more personal. 'You ask me how to pray,' said Jesus of Nazareth. 'Well, when you pray say this, "Our Father..."'

God is an intimate relative, a parent, a friend, a mother or father. That prayer – the Lord's Prayer – is said so often by so many that no one anymore notices how personal it is, how intimate a conversation.

Jesus told his friends stories about prayer: for example the way that you have to keep at it, to persist. It's like you've run out of cash late one night and the ATM outside the bank is bust, so you knock on the door of a friend who's asleep in bed. Then you call their mobile, then you throw stones at their window. God is that friend. Keep bugging her until she wakes up, until she lends you the cash you need.

We may think of our prayers as discreet, individual gobbets, millions of them rising like invisible helium balloons to some hidden call centre where their messages are decoded. But maybe, instead, every prayer is the same prayer: all of life the one prayer, one eternal desperate longing through all of history and all of geography. The longing for things to be different.

'Prayer is translation,' said Leonard Cohen. 'A man translates himself into a child asking for all there is in a language he has barely mastered.'[2]

Prayer is how we wake God up.

But if you think God never sleeps, then prayer is how we wake ourselves up.

29

KNOW YOUR PLACE

Ever since humans exchanged a mobile, hunter-gatherer existence for a settled agricultural one, location – place – has become more significant. As hamlets have morphed into villages, towns, cities and nation states, place and identity have grown progressively more intertwined. Many people still see themselves bound to where they were born, or where they live.

In *The Road to Somewhere*, David Goodhart says that these people look at the world from 'Somewhere'. These 'Somewheres' include those who are 'rooted and usually have "ascribed" identities – Scottish farmer, working-class Geordie, Cornish housewife – based on group belonging and particular places'.[1] They represent around half of the UK population.

But culture and society in the UK, North America and many European countries, he says, has become dominated by a smaller, more liberal, more mobile, globalised group that he calls 'Anywheres'. In the UK, these people 'tend to do well at school and then usually move from home to a residential university in their late teens and on to a career in the professions that might take them to London or even abroad for a year or two'. They represent barely a quarter of the population, but for the last twenty-five years they, and their values, have set the political and cultural agenda. This may have something to do with a core group of 'Somewheres' feeling uncomfortable with the speed of change, and worrying that they're being left behind.

To divide populations into such loose groupings risks caricature, and Goodhart confesses that 'few of us belong completely to either group... there is a large minority of "Inbetweeners"'. All the same, there's something acute about his observations.

The social liberalism, openness to new ideas and tolerance of diversity which characterises 'Anywheres' is admirable, but there remains enormous value in holding on to, or putting down, roots in a place. The shepherd and writer Amanda Owen talks about how a group of hill sheep in the Yorkshire Dales will stick to their own patch of moorland – as their mothers did and their lambs will continue to – despite their being no boundaries to stop them from roaming. She says: 'The word for this is "heafing". The sheep are "heafed" or "hefted" or "hoofed" on to their part of the moors.'[2]

With her husband and nine children, she farms Ravenseat, 2,000 acres with 1,000 sheep, alongside chickens, pigs, cows and horses. She talks of the spiritual rootedness she feels to the place: 'For me the winter is when I really feel a special connection with the land... There's a cold lifelessness in the earth, everything is so raw and quiet out on the moors. You can see for miles, heather, peat haggs and big skies overhead... To the untrained eye they might say it is a dark, barren and featureless landscape but for me it's not at all foreboding. It is where I feel at home, the sheep are heafed to Ravenseat, and so too I am attached to the place by an invisible bond.'[3]

We may have, in Goodhart's words, 'portable, "achieved" identities', but there's a profound satisfaction in finding a location with meaning. Even if it's your bedroom. At the turn of the seventeenth and eighteenth centuries, Xavier de Maistre wrote *A Journey Around My Room* in which, wearing pink and blue pyjamas, he would move from his bed to the sofa, and from his sofa to his desk as if he was embarking on a voyage of intrepid discovery.

Location means far more than geography. Robert Macfarlane writes: 'What we bloodlessly call "place" is to young children a wild compound of dream, spell and substance: place is somewhere they are always "in", never "on".'[4]

Maybe it's possible to be anywhere but, at the same time, in place.

30

The best things in life
are not Things

The print-run of the IKEA catalogue is twice that of the Bible. Furniture is more popular than faith. And usually more functional. But there is the odd overlap in the Venn diagram of holy writ and home improvements.

When the sustainability manager of the Swedish superstore announced that the world may have finally reached 'peak stuff', he was cottoning on to something Nazareth's most famous carpenter spoke about: 'For what shall it profit someone if he gains the whole world yet loses his own soul?'

In the world's richest countries, most of us have a lot of stuff. We like to get things. To own them and keep them, and then upgrade them. It takes a wise person to know when they have enough.

Some of our stuff is highly prized for different reasons.

That dog-eared ticket stub from a night we'll never forget.

The car we could never afford. But did.

The ring that once belonged to a lost relative.

We treasure them. Yes. For what they're worth? No.

A cynic, said an Oscar Wilde character, 'knows the price of everything, and the value of nothing'. It's impossible to price things that can't be bought or sold. The preciousness of some objects doesn't reside in their quality as objects. It's not their *thingness* that enchants us. It's something less tangible – memory, journey, association.

The American humorist Art Buchwald put it like this: 'The best things in life aren't things.' He wasn't joking.

What we value ultimately, aren't possessions at all. They're things we can never actually own...

That first, hesitant kiss.

A child's look of amazement.

Finally understanding something.

The trust of a good friend.

Knowing you've been forgiven.

The kindness of a stranger.

What keeps us going are priceless imponderables, like love, joy, beauty, knowledge.

Bean grinder or fancy cappuccino machine? Who cares, if we never wake up and smell the coffee.

31

Let the music
take you

The screwdriver has not yet been invented which can unscrew the inscrutable. Words only reach so far in trying to describe the indescribable. Some days they are the best help we can find. Other days, we need something else.

Music is one of those something elses. A tune can carry freight. Music, said the composer and conductor Leonard Bernstein, 'can name the unnameable and communicate the unknowable'. And depending on who is composing or performing it, it can name different unnameable things. Talking about three of the 'greats' in classical music, Douglas Adams put it like this: 'Beethoven tells you what it's like to be Beethoven and Mozart tells you what it's like to be human. Bach tells you what it's like to be the universe.'[1]

Music can tell you things by taking you places. It can transport you to heaven, whether you believe in heaven or not. And that's the holy grail for songwriters and composers. David Bowie tried to explain: 'Searching for music is like searching for God. They're very similar. There's an effort to reclaim the unsayable, the unmentionable, the unseeable, the unspeakable. All of these things come into being for a composer, a writer.'[2]

For instance, when we hear – when we *feel*

– those left-hand piano chords in Gospel music, our faith is more likely to be stirred than by reciting a shrinkwrapped creed in a religious service. Or take Soul music – that mystical meld of Gospel and rhythm and blues. We call it Soul, but it's physical too, its visceral rhythm hauling you to your feet, and driving you to the dance floor. It's body *and* spirit.

Or the act of singing, how you can lose yourself in the melody, how the words no longer matter, how it's subsumed into a feeling of connection. 'Singing,' says Joseph Shabalala of South Africa's choral group Ladysmith Black Mambazo, 'is just like kneeling down and praying.'[3]

Over the centuries, religious institutions like the Church have become obsessed with words, attempting to tie down the mystery of existence in polysyllables. Why try so hard when polyphony – that densely woven texture of voice and instrument – does a much better job of embodying that *mysterium tremendum*.

When you hear a piano playing, especially those sad, indigo blue phrases that come from the heart of the Mississippi Delta, or when a choral bass drone rolls around the barrel vault of a church, that's a sonic landscape where you can begin to believe that God is in the house.

'ACTIVISM IS MY RENT FOR LIVING ON THIS PLANET.'[1]

ALICE WALKER

Take the road
less travelled

William Dodd, an obscure eighteenth-century English clergyman, built up gambling debts, was publically disgraced and barely merits a toenail on a footnote in history. But his conviction, and death by hanging, sparked one of the best-remembered sayings of his properly famous friend, Dr Samuel Johnson.

Facing his grisly end at the gallows, Dodd delivered a sermon, which, it was noted, sounded suspiciously like the work of his celebrated pal. Dr Johnson rebuffed the notion with this reply: 'Depend upon it, sir, when a man knows he is to be hanged in a fortnight, it concentrates his mind wonderfully.'

True enough. There's nothing like the knowledge of impending death to clarify the thinking. Death does more than remind us to get our affairs in order, it frames our days. Puts our life in a different perspective. It invites us to ask what we really want from the time that we are alive. And sometimes that leads to a sense of regret – about the choices we made or what we did with our time. We might even remember reaching a crossroads, see ourselves standing there while deciding which route to take... and wonder wistfully at the road we didn't follow.

Nowhere are those regrets more obvious than in the care home, where people live out their final days. In her conversations with patients in palliative care over a period of twelve years, Australian nurse, Bronnie Ware, noticed certain common threads. People wished that they'd let themselves be happier in life. They regretted losing touch with friends. They felt sad for the times when they hadn't said what they'd been thinking – been unable to express their true feelings. Men, especially, said if they had their time again they wouldn't spend so much of it at work. And all of these many disappointments were summed up in the most common regret

of all: 'I wish I'd had the courage to live a life true to myself, not the life others expected of me.'[1]

If it's not the gallows that will concentrate our minds about life, it may well be a serious illness or a traumatic life event that is the epiphany casting our ordinary days in a new light. Towards the end of his life, Raymond Carver, one of the most revered of twentieth-century American writers, wrote a short poem, 'Gravy', which is inscribed on his tombstone. It captures the story of a man nearly dead from alcohol abuse at forty who then 'changed his ways somehow'. The rest of his life, he wrote, was 'pure gravy'.[2] It was Carver's own story and, although he died from lung cancer only ten years later, they were years of sobriety, love and happiness. He had reached a junction, and taken a different road. He had no regrets.

We may recall decisions we faced at major crossroads in our lives but forget the minor ones – the myriad intersections of B roads and cycle paths and holloways that form the ordnance survey map of any given day. The choices we're faced with, which ask us who we want to be.

Asked to give a speech for the graduates of Syracuse University, the novelist George Saunders reflected on how, as we get older, we're invited to wonder how we might have lived differently. It wasn't strange jobs or disabling illness that he wished he'd missed out on, but how he had responded to a small, shy stranger, briefly part of his class at school, routinely ignored and often teased. Her hurt look haunted his memory. When he asked himself why he still thinks about her forty years on, he knows that it's about regret: 'What I regret most in my life are failures of kindness. Those moments when another human being was there, in front of me, suffering, and I responded... sensibly. Reservedly. Mildly.'[3]

34

Remember you are dust

We're physical people, with physical needs in a physical universe. Material boys and girls we are. But that's not all. Mind and soul and spirit are difficult to define, and harder to locate, but the idea that they are part of our makeup needs to be taken seriously. All the same, we are bodies, on earth.

Earth. The word is rich, crumbly, fertile, organic, alive. It's solid, dependable, firm, foundational, nutritional. You can grow in earth, build with it, shape it and fire it, tunnel through it, hollow it out. The earth is our home, we are earthy, grounded, rooted people.

That makes our bodies significant. They're not simply temporary shells for the soul to live in, as if the soul or spirit was the real thing and the body simply packaging – a popular idea in religious circles. The psychologist Guy Claxton, in *The Wayward Mind*, says there's an inclination to think of our souls as a 'buried scrap of divinity, the immaculate memento of [God's] glory, which [he has] hidden in every human heart'.[1]

But you can't divorce the soul or spirit from the rest of who we are, he says. It's intertwined with the rest of us. It's about being joined up with the air we breathe, the food we eat, the culture that nurtures us, the families who raise us and – if you're so inclined – the divinity within us. It's part of the 'relationship with *this* world of wood and gristle and fellow feeling'.[2]

Our identities – the heart of us – are embodied, embedded, incarnated. The fact that we are earthed is the reason that place, genes, family, ethnicity, nation, culture and friendship are elemental to us.

We are extraordinarily complex: a bundle of logic, instinct, animal urges, emotions, calculation and gut belief which defy reason. The whole of our being is responding to a mass of stimuli including the cycles and rhythms of nature. William Wordsworth was onto this in his 'Lines Written a Few Miles above Tintern Abbey':

A presence that disturbs me with the joy
Of elevated thoughts; a sense sublime
Of something far more deeply interfused...
... A motion and a spirit, that impels
All thinking things, all objects of all thought,
And rolls through all things...[3]

Maybe the earth has soul too. Maybe we're closer than we know – something captured for Christians in the liturgy of Ash Wednesday as they hear the words: 'Remember you are dust and to dust you shall return.'

If soul, spirit, mind, body and earth are so entangled, why make a clinical distinction between flesh and spirit, between secular and sacred?

Being properly alive, wrote Nina Cassian, the Romanian poet and composer, is to transcend those boundaries, to 'feel light gliding across the cornea like the train of a dress'. At which point, she reckoned, 'your shoulder blades will ache for the want of wings'.[4]

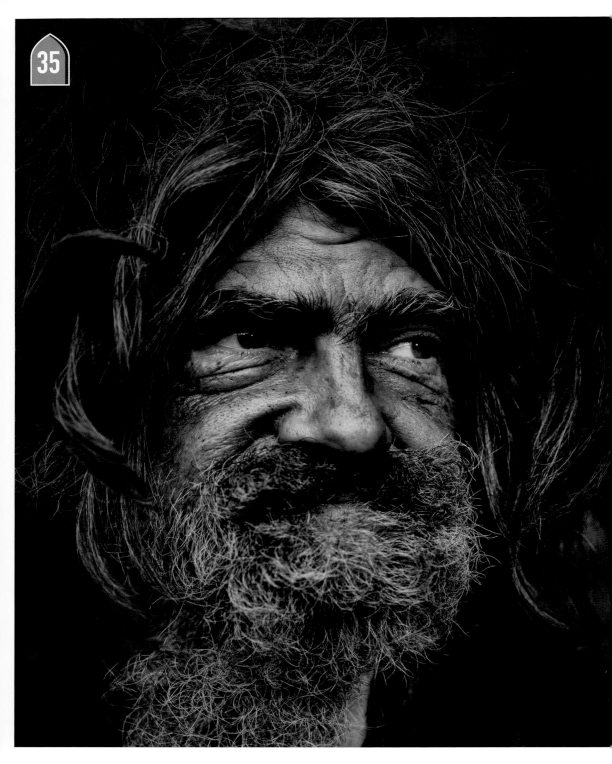

35

Everybody Hurts

Shit happens. It's like gravity, or the second law of thermodynamics. It affects all of us. We can't avoid pain and misfortune. We might suffer from a broken heart or a broken leg. Either way, we suffer.

We may get hurt because of something we've done, deliberately, or by accident. Or it may be someone else's doing, on purpose or by mishap. Or it may be no one's doing. Shit might just happen, through earthquake, cancer, being in the wrong place at the wrong time.

Who's to blame? God? The Devil? Fate? The alignment of the planets? The government? Often, our pain has a cause that we can point to, and occasionally someone is culpable. But that cause is not the reason for our hurt. To comment – say, when a child dies, or someone's life is ruined – that it is *meant to be*, is just cruel.

Philosophers and theologians have tried to find a reason why we suffer. But no one seems to have got much beyond the conclusion that shit happens, and that this may be quite random. Bad luck. In Buddhism, life *is* suffering. Take up your cross, says Jesus, in the Christian tradition. We look around us and cannot deny that pain and loss marks all our lives – and with no evident rhyme or reason.

The alternative is bleak. To believe in an omni-god – an all-knowing, all-powerful cosmic project manager, who organises individual pain and pleasure as part of a universal scheme – is to be stuck with a dark, monstrous divinity of epic proportions. And it makes us into puppets, dancing on strings to a tortured, gothic tune.

Is there another way of looking at this? Alfred North Whitehead, the twentieth-century English mathematician and philosopher, talked instead of a 'fluent' God who joins with us in the process of life. God, he said, is our 'great companion – the fellow-sufferer who understands'.[1] Someone, as the Hebrew prophet Isaiah put it, who joins in 'bearing our griefs and carrying our sorrows'. Someone that people in the Christian tradition recognise in Jesus of Nazareth.

Shit is not meant to happen. Bad things are not good. But we are not alone. Remarkably, people can often emerge from wreckage not of their own making bruised, but stronger – supported by friends, family and the kindness of strangers, in whom some people recognise the presence of some loving companion.

In their song 'Everybody Hurts',[2] REM have a point. You are not alone. Hold on.

36

Experience others

'Ouch, that must have hurt!'

'I know what you mean.'

'If I were you...'

Human beings are, supremely, imaginative creatures. And the moral heart of the imagination is the ability to understand what it's like to be someone else. To have *empathy*. To walk a mile in someone else's shoes, as the saying goes.

If you've been struck down by serious illness; if you've been elated by good news; if you're bewildered by what's happening to you – then you'll hope that someone else will understand. And be there for you.

'Imagination is not only the uniquely human capacity to envision that which is not, and therefore the fount of all invention and innovation,' says J. K. Rowling. 'In its arguably most transformative and revelatory capacity, it is the power that enables us to empathise with humans whose experiences we have never shared.'[1]

This ability to identify with what other people are going through, or to be able to figure out what it might be like should something happen to them, is the backbone of a good life. Unless we know what someone else is facing, how can we help them effectively? It's part of our common humanity.

'Each one of us has lived through some devastation, some loneliness, some weather superstorm or spiritual superstorm,' says the writer Maya Angelou. 'When we look at each other we must say, I understand. I understand how you feel because I have been there myself. We must support each other and empathise with each other because each of us is more alike than we are unalike.'[2]

It makes sense that writers of fiction get the idea of empathy. How else can they create plausible characters? They have to get under their skins. The novelist Jonathan Franzen points out that empathy is not about some vague sense of fellow feeling with the rest of the world. The rubber hits the road when we feel what it's like to be one other real person. 'Love is about bottomless empathy, born out of the heart's revelation that another person is every bit as real as you are,' says Franzen. 'And this is why love, as I understand it, is always specific. Trying to love all of humanity may be a worthy endeavour, but, in a funny way, it keeps the focus on the self, on the self's own moral or spiritual well-being. Whereas, to love a specific person, and to identify with his or her struggles and joys as if they were your own, you have to surrender some of your self.'[3]

This idea of selflessness – of giving up something of yourself in order to share in the life of someone else – is ancient wisdom. When Jesus said: 'Love thy neighbour as thyself,' he was tapping into a revered tradition. He was probably quoting from the ancient Hebrew book, Leviticus, written up to 600 years before. There are equivalents of the saying in Chinese, Indian, Egyptian and Arabic spiritual teaching. You could say that it's the kernel of all religion.

37

Be foolish

No one knows for sure if Leonardo da Vinci painted *Salvator Mundi*, and when it was first 'discovered' in 1958 it was sold for $200 (£145). Nearly sixty years later, after restoration, the painting came on the market again. It sold for $450 million (£327.5 million), the most expensive work of art in history at the time.

In a market economy everything has a price. Supply and demand are in charge. There are barely twenty works by da Vinci in existence, so if one comes on the market demand is stratospheric. But who has that kind of money... and what else you could do with $450 million?

'Drawing is based upon perspective,' said Leonardo, also a brilliant mathematician, 'which is nothing else than a thorough knowledge of the function of the eye.' Today, medical technology gives us an even more thorough knowledge of the function of the eye but an estimated 36 million people in the world have no function. They are blind. Another 217 million are visually impaired. Cataracts, which account for half of all blindness, can be treated with surgery for around £24 per person. You can buy da Vinci's *Salvator Mundi* or you can restore the sight of 14 million people. What will you do?

Living and breathing inside a market economy, we absorb its language and world view. We think about how 'hard' we can make our money work, the best return on our investment. But for all its benefits, one of the downsides of market capitalism is that it persuades us to quantify everything. To price things that are priceless.

How do you value a work of art? Come to that, how do you value family life? Or public service? How do you value the time spent stopping to talk with a neighbour, or volunteering on a school trip? The cultural critic Lewis Hyde explored this question in *The Gift*, pointing out, for instance, that art and creativity often don't fit the world of market forces. Sometimes, he writes, it's better to see life as a gift than a commercial transaction. He cites the 'gift exchange' culture of some ancient societies, where it was understood that everyone participates in a cycle of giving, and the act of giving is an act of faith, a kind of abandonment. You cannot control the 'returns'. But it's 'when a part of the self is given away,' he writes, 'that community appears'.[1]

In a culture where everything is weighed, measured and has a price tag attached, this seems daft. But life is full of counter-cultural figures who have stepped out of the mainstream to challenge prevailing wisdom. Painters, poets or novelists, for example, who are compelled to follow their art, but whose work may never be acclaimed, and whose books may never be balanced. Nuns or monks who take vows of poverty or chastity, resisting accepted norms in favour of 'unproductive' and inefficient lives: in favour of that 'condition of complete simplicity', which T. S. Eliot said, costs 'not less than everything'.[2]

Sometimes the sensible decision is daft, and the foolish choice is wise. The wisdom of this world, as the first-century Christian teacher Paul put it, may be foolishness.

Someone somewhere has invested $450 million of their money in Leonardo's *Salvator Mundi*. The sensible thing would be to keep it in a safe for a few years before selling it on at a vast profit. But perhaps they'll anonymously donate the painting to a public gallery, with the only condition that it's open to all the public every day of the week.

Now, that would be daft.

38

There is
no such thing as
good grief

For Grief

When you lose someone you love,
Your life becomes strange,
The ground beneath you becomes fragile,
Your thoughts make your eyes unsure;
And some dead echo drags your voice down
Where words have no confidence
Your heart has grown heavy with loss;
And though this loss has wounded others too,
No one knows what has been taken from you
When the silence of absence deepens.
Flickers of guilt kindle regret
For all that was left unsaid or undone.
There are days when you wake up happy;
Again inside the fullness of life,
Until the moment breaks
And you are thrown back
Onto the black tide of loss.
Days when you have your heart back,
You are able to function well
Until in the middle of work or encounter,
Suddenly with no warning,
You are ambushed by grief.
It becomes hard to trust yourself.
All you can depend on now is that
Sorrow will remain faithful to itself.
More than you, it knows its way
And will find the right time
To pull and pull the rope of grief
Until that coiled hill of tears
Has reduced to its last drop.
Gradually, you will learn acquaintance
With the invisible form of your departed;
And when the work of grief is done,
The wound of loss will heal
And you will have learned
To wean your eyes
From that gap in the air
And be able to enter the hearth
In your soul where your loved one
Has awaited your return
All the time.[1]

JOHN O'DONOHUE

39

Breathe in

Air is our medium, like water is for fish. We can't live without it, but we take it pretty much for granted. Unless, for some reason, we can't breathe – if we find ourselves submerged in water; if we're choking, or having an asthma attack.

We notice air when it's moving, when we feel the breeze, or when a sudden gust bowls a dustbin down the street. And air carries other things with it: the waft of perfume from someone's neck; the tang of brine from the ocean; the haze of woodsmoke from a cottage chimney.

But air is mostly about breath. It's what keeps us alive. When we breathe in, we exchange the oxygen for carbon dioxide and then breathe out. It's part of an unconscious, life-giving rhythm. When we inhale, the air travels down our windpipe and into our lungs, it ends up in air sacs with thin walls called alveoli, from where the oxygen is absorbed into the bloodstream. Air becomes an indivisible part of us.

The early chapters of *Genesis*, the first book of the Bible, picture air in a more mystical way. At the dawn of creation, a divine wind swept over the face of the deep. The Hebrew word used for wind is also used for breath – so God *breathed* the world into being. She *exhaled* it into existence. God breathed life into the nostrils of humankind.

The first thing the first human did was to breathe in – and be inspired. It's pretty much the first thing any of us do when we're born.

We inhale through all our senses, taking in smells, sights, sounds, tastes, textures. We absorb what's in the air: ideas, stories, images, music, styles, attitudes, behaviour. This *in*-spiration shapes who we are and what we do. And who we are inspires others. We breathe in and breathe out. All of us, together.

In. Out. In. Out. Noticing our breathing, becoming mindful of it, helps us notice everything else. Thinking of nothing else is how we can think of everything.

Inspiration fills our lungs, but also our mind, our heart, our spirit. What inspires us becomes who we are. Breathing out, we become what we do.

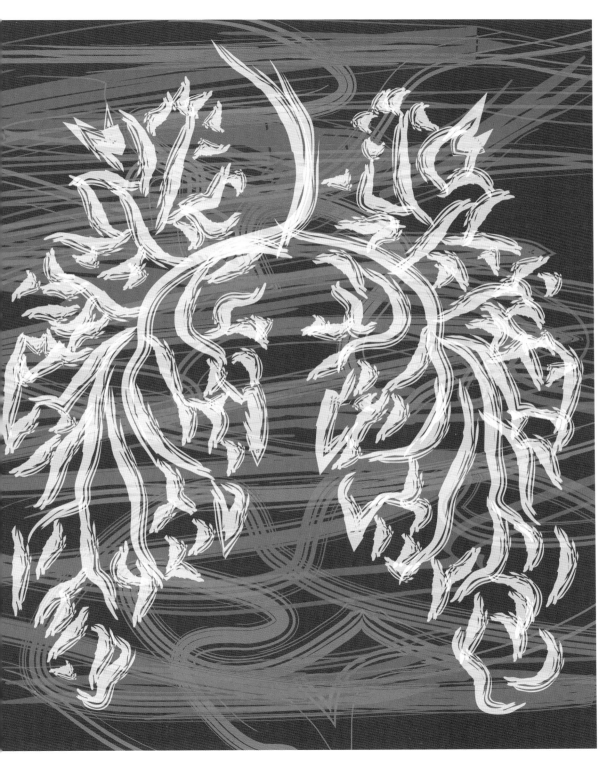

40

'This being human is a
guest house...'

THE GUEST HOUSE

This being human is a guest house.
Every morning a new arrival.

A joy, a depression, a meanness,
some momentary awareness comes
as an unexpected visitor.

Welcome and entertain them all!
Even if they are a crowd of sorrows,
who violently sweep your house
empty of its furniture,
still, treat each guest honorably.
He may be clearing you out
for some new delight.

The dark thought, the shame, the malice,
meet them at the door laughing and
invite them in.

Be grateful for whatever comes,
because each has been sent
as a guide from beyond.[1]

JALALUDDIN RUMI

How do the words of an obscure Islamic scholar, born in Afghanistan in 1207, who lived and died in Turkey, still ring true across all those centuries? How can someone writing in Persian 800 years ago be a bestselling poet at the beginning of the twenty-first century?

Perhaps it's because Jalaluddin Rumi understood what today we call 'mindfulness'. That our attitude to the events that shape each day – however small, however great – will define what shape they make of our lives.

Whatever happens, we'll have guests today. Bringing joy or bringing sadness. They don't wait to be invited in. And there's more to each one than we know...

41

JOIN THE RESISTANCE

The singer–songwriter Luis Enrique Mejía Godoy composed the following verses using the words of Tomás Borge, who was imprisoned and tortured under the Somoza regime, and became Interior Minister of Nicaragua after the Sandinista revolution in 1979:

REVENGE

My personal revenge will be your children's right to schooling and to flowers.
My personal revenge will be this song bursting for you with no more fears.

My personal revenge will be to make you see the goodness in my people's eyes, implacable in combat always generous and firm in victory.

My personal revenge will be to greet you 'Good morning!' in streets with no beggars, when instead of locking you inside they say, 'Don't look so sad.'
When you, the torturer, daren't lift your head,

My personal revenge will be to give you these hands you once ill-treated with all their tenderness intact.[1]

If a picture was once worth a thousand words, today it's a photo. Sometimes an image can transfix the public imagination by capturing in a single frame something about the human condition which a library of words can't articulate. Something, for example, like the quiet resistance of ordinary people.

When in the spring of 2017 a young political activist from Birmingham, Saffiyah Khan, put herself in harm's way to support a woman wearing a hijab who was being menaced by a member of the English Defence League, she had no idea that she was about to experience viral fame. A photograph of Saffiyah, calm and smiling in the face of a furious male opponent, went around the world. 'You don't scare me,' she seems to be saying, 'I have strength too.' 'Sometimes,' she told reporters later, 'it's more important to smile than to shout.'

The image resonated with that of a young American woman, Iesha L. Evans, standing defiant and alone in the middle of the road, elegant in a long dress, facing down a line of heavily armed riot police at a Black Lives Matters protest in 2016. Further back too, it recalls an image from Tiananmen Square in 1989: 'Tank Man', or 'The Unknown Protestor' as he has become known, holds a shopping bag in one hand while holding up a formidable force of Chinese tanks with the other.

Images of unlikely daring, even foolishness, by people resisting the presence of a world they do not believe in, people standing firm whatever the odds. Captured on film, they draw a fleeting fame; but every day countless others too are resisting the odds – refusing to bow the knee to oppressive governments,

or political bullies, or inhuman laws. Dancing to a different drummer, they constitute a quiet, continuous, disruptive resistance. An alternative narrative in history.

History sometimes defines people with this kind of counter-cultural fearlessness as heroes. Religions may call them saints: people who choose another way of seeing life. While religions often value saintliness over subversion, true goodness may be less about piety and purity, and more about a defiance which draws on a mysterious inner strength that we may never even know we have.

On 1 December 1955, a bus driver in Montgomery Alabama demanded that Rosa Parks give up her seat for a white man. Something told Parks she shouldn't: 'When that white driver stepped back toward us, when he waved his hand and ordered us up and out of our seats, I felt a determination cover my body like a quilt on a winter night.'[2]

She was arrested, placed in custody and found guilty in court, but her resistance sparked the Montgomery Bus Boycott and, within a year, the US Supreme Court ruled that bus segregation was unconstitutional.

Sometimes our resistance comes with a smile, a twinkle in the eye of a storm. The theologian Walter Wink tells this story of apartheid South Africa: 'Desmond Tutu walked by a construction site on a temporary sidewalk the width of one person. A white man appeared at the other end, recognised Tutu, and said, "I don't make way for gorillas." At which Tutu stepped aside, made a deep sweeping gesture, and said, "Ah, yes, but I do."'[3]

42

Duty calls

Growing up most of us had to negotiate a bewildering labyrinth of expectations, often peculiar to our family, school and peer group.

Eat all your greens. Be in bed before ten. Don't slam the door. Do your chores. Let Granny give you a kiss. Look at me when I'm talking to you. Always throw your litter in the bin. Whatever you do, don't ever call Richard, Dick.

Some of them were rules, some of them were for our own good, some of them were just good manners. But they were expectations, usually imposed rather than self-generated. And sometimes they felt like arbitrary commands – prompting the dragging of feet, and a sulk the size of Wales.

Some obligations continue into our adult lives – in fact duties and responsibilities multiply: family, friends, work, community...

Again, they often carry the burden of other people's expectations: 'You really ought to...'; 'You should...'

For some of us, this breeds resentment. We feel pushed into a corner. We do our duty, but with bad grace. On the other hand, we may take our obligations so seriously that we become overburdened and leave no time for our own wellbeing – suffering from an unhealthy 'hardening of the oughteries'.

Nevertheless, we can't live lives of isolation. Having family, friends, colleagues, neighbours, means give and take. Wrapped up in all this are those things like taking your turn on the coffee rota, visiting a neighbour who's poorly, or phoning your auntie. Some people call it kindness. We're not obliged to do any of this – it's not exactly our duty. But if we don't, then we lose touch, grow lonely, shrink a little – and, as a result, humanity's diminished just that tiny bit.

Institutions and organisations are often taken to task about their 'duty of care'. Good call. Ultimately, care is at the very heart of obligation. The novelist Albert Camus once said: 'I only know of one duty, and that is to love.'

The Trappist monk Thomas Merton suggested that if we try and love people first, then liking them and doing our duty to them comes easier: 'If we wait for some people to become agreeable or attractive before we begin to love them, we will never begin. If we are content to give them a cold impersonal "charity" that is merely a matter of obligation, we will not trouble to understand them or to sympathise with them at all.'[1]

Obligation isn't a one-way street. At best, our responsibilities spring from mutuality – rooted in the reality of living cheek by jowl with other people. In the old story of Cain and Abel, Cain is asked the whereabouts of his missing brother. Guilty, and cornered, he retorts: 'Am I my brother's keeper?' The answer is 'Yes'.

We don't use the term so much these days, but an old way of expressing our thanks was to say, 'much obliged'. Put another way: 'I owe you one.' We don't, of course. Not exactly. But then again, we do. It's about duty.

43

Do good
anyway

People are illogical, unreasonable, and self-centred. Love them anyway.

If you do good, people will accuse you of selfish ulterior motives. Do good anyway.

If you are successful, you will win false friends and true enemies. Succeed anyway.

The good you do today will be forgotten tomorrow. Do good anyway.

Honesty and frankness make you vulnerable. Be honest and frank anyway.

The biggest men and women with the biggest ideas can be shot down by the smallest men and women with the smallest minds. Think big anyway.

People favour underdogs but follow only top dogs. Fight for a few underdogs anyway.

What you spend years building may be destroyed overnight. Build anyway.

People really need help but may attack you if you help them. Help people anyway.

Give the world the best you have and you'll get kicked in the teeth. Give the world the best you have anyway.

It's sometimes called 'Do Good Anyway' – or just 'Anyway' – and attributed to Mother Teresa, the Catholic nun who founded the Sisters of Charity and worked among the poorest people in the Indian city of Kolkata. After her death in 1997, some say it was found above the desk in the small room she had lived in from the 1950s. Others that the words hung on the wall of Shishu Bhavan, one of the homes she founded for abandoned children.

In fact, this poem in praise of resilience in the face of setbacks, of mutuality in the face of hostility, is based on *The Paradoxical Commandments* written in 1968 by nineteen-year-old American, Kent Keith,[1] in a booklet for student leaders. Like a lot of inspirational writing the material has been adapted for different audiences, but the association with Mother Teresa propelled it to a global audience.

Kent Keith had no idea of any of this until, in a meeting after Mother Teresa's death, 'a poem she had written' was delivered in tribute. He recognised most of the words as his own, from more than thirty years before. Later, he discovered other versions but his essential idea was usually retained: We find meaning when we love and help people, no matter who they may be, or how difficult they may be. We find meaning by loving and helping them anyway.

44

God Is Not
A Christian
(or Muslim, or Jew,
or Buddhist, or Sikh,
or Hindu, or agnostic,
or atheist)

The Hebrew scriptures came up with the idea that women and men are some kind of copy of the divine. 'So God created man in his own image,' reads the seventeenth-century King James edition of the Bible. 'Male and female created he them...'[1]

However, throughout history we've tended to create God in *our* image. And, without anthropomorphic language, how else do we picture the divine? A popular childhood version features God as elderly and bearded, balancing on a celestial cloud. But there are grown-up versions too, in which, as religions become more sophisticated, they overstate their backstage access to heaven. They make exclusive truth claims about God and dismiss those of other traditions. The impression is conveyed that God has signed up to their own particular club which has a monopoly on the truth.

But what we see depends on where we stand. The faith we follow is, overwhelmingly, informed by where in the world we happened to have grown up. Rosa, born in Italy and raised Catholic, would almost certainly have been Muslim if she'd been born in Pakistan. Akio, raised by his Japanese family in devotion to the invisible spiritual beings of Shinto, would have been Hindu if he'd been born in India.

We all tend to be fearful and suspicious of the other and religion is no exception. An admission of doubt is a kind of defeat, the best way to protect one's own religious story is to attack rival stories. But what's reflected back at us in the divine, depends on the angle of our view. 'God is like a mirror,' said the rabbi Harold S. Kushner. 'The mirror never changes, but everybody who looks at it sees something different.'[2]

While there is a surprising degree of convergence on the mysteries of prayer and meditation, we should admit, says Desmond Tutu, that on many questions faiths take different views: 'We should in humility and joyfulness acknowledge that the supernatural and divine reality we all worship in some form or other transcends all our particular categories of thought and imagining, and that because the divine – however named, however apprehended or conceived – is infinite and we are forever finite, we shall never comprehend the divine completely.'[3]

But rather than be fearful of difference we can embrace it, he says: 'We should seek to share all insights we can and be ready to learn, for instance, from the techniques of the spiritual life that are available in religions other than our own. It is interesting that most religions have a transcendent reference point, a *mysterium tremendum*, that comes to be known by deigning to reveal itself, himself, herself, to humanity; that the transcendent reality is compassionate and concerned; that human beings are creatures of this supreme, supra mundane reality in some way, with a high destiny that hopes for an everlasting life lived in close association with the divine, either as absorbed without distinction between creature and creator, between the divine and human, or in a wonderful intimacy which still retains the distinctions between these two orders of reality.'[4]

45

Keep the
doubt

Faith is sometimes misunderstood. It carries echoes of certitude, belief, conviction. But for many people that's not really what faith is about. It's much more fragile than that.

It's often said that the opposite of faith is doubt. Richard Holloway, former Bishop of Edinburgh, disagrees. 'The opposite of faith is not doubt, but certainty,' he says. 'Where you have certainty, you don't need faith.'[1]

Faith comes into play when you can't be absolutely sure. When you put your life in the hands of a surgeon, for example. A good outcome is statistically probable, but not certain. And there's probably even less verifiable data to rely on when it comes to asking why there's something rather than nothing, or whether there's some presence behind or within, or beyond what we can physically see.

Faith is an experiment, a wager. Holloway says: 'Faith, by definition, always implies doubt.' Certainty does not. Certainty is cut and dried, black and white.

The poet John Keats believed that doubt was a virtue. He called it 'negative capability'. He was talking about artists who pursue beauty even if it ultimately led them to intellectual confusion or uncertainty. An individual

demonstrated such negative capability when he or she was 'capable of being in uncertainty, mystery, doubt, without irritably reaching after fact or reason'.[2]

It's important to live comfortably with doubt and uncertainty. Because, ironically, a discomfort with the unprovable can give rise to dangerous certainties. Holloway writes: 'What do you do if you can no longer live with the doubt that is co-active with faith? You try to cure yourself. And the best cure for doubt is over-conviction... it is like the refusal to let pity weaken you in face of your enemy. Doubt, like pity, erodes certainty.'[3]

Institutions, such as religions and political parties, tend to usher their members from faith into certainty: into dogma and ideology. Certainty is the shadow side of faith – the Devil on its shoulder.

Anne Lamott writes: 'I have a lot of faith. But I am also afraid a lot, and have no real certainty about anything... Certainty is missing the point entirely. Faith includes noticing the mess, the emptiness and discomfort, and letting it be there until some light returns.'[4]

Have faith, keep the doubt.

Faith...

... ENLIGHTENS THE PATH BEHIND YOU,
BUT AS A RULE, IN FRONT OF YOU
IT IS STILL DARK.[1]

Richard Rohr

... IS NOT AN EPIDURAL.
FAITH IS A MIDWIFE.[2]

Brené Brown

Hope...

... IMAGINES THE FUTURE AND THEN ACTS
AS IF THAT FUTURE IS IRRESISTIBLE.[1]

Walter Wink

... IS A SENSE OF THE GRAND MYSTERY OF
IT ALL, THE KNOWLEDGE THAT WE DON'T
KNOW HOW IT WILL TURN OUT, THAT
ANYTHING IS POSSIBLE.[2]

Rebecca Solnit

Love...

... ALL GOD'S CREATION, THE WHOLE
AND EVERY GRAIN OF SAND OF IT. LOVE
EVERY LEAF, EVERY RAY OF GOD'S
LIGHT. LOVE THE ANIMALS, LOVE THE
PLANTS, LOVE EVERYTHING. IF YOU
LOVE EVERYTHING, YOU WILL PERCEIVE
THE DIVINE MYSTERY IN THINGS. ONCE
YOU PERCEIVE IT, YOU WILL BEGIN TO
COMPREHEND IT BETTER EVERY DAY.
AND YOU WILL COME AT LAST TO LOVE
THE WHOLE WORLD WITH AN
ALL-EMBRACING LOVE.[1]

Fyodor Dostoevsky

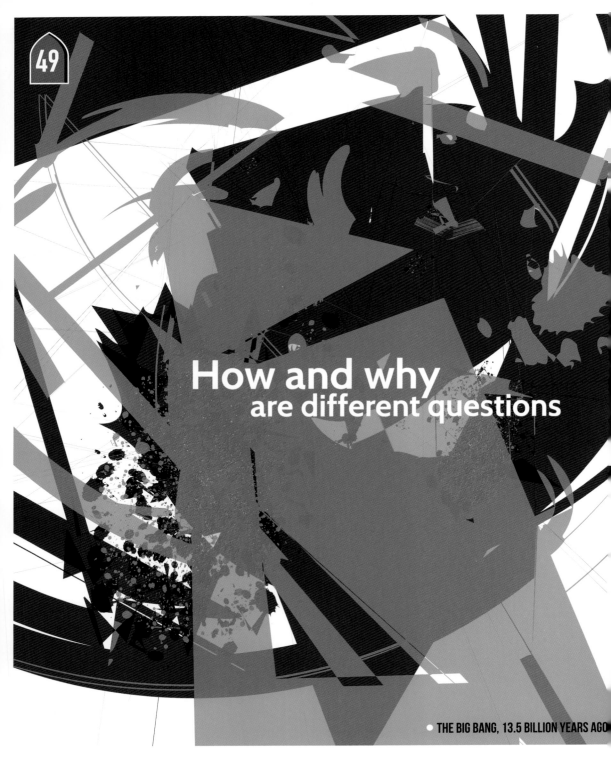

49

How and why
are different questions

● THE BIG BANG, 13.5 BILLION YEARS AGO

It started about 13.5 billion years ago.
It being something rather than nothing.
It being the event we call the Big Bang
which, from the middle of nowhere,
produced this small corner of somewhere.

It being matter. It being energy, time and
space.

It being the story which began with 'In the
Beginning', when 'God created the heaven
and the earth, and called the light Day, and
the darkness Night, and the evening and the
morning were the first day.'[1]

Not long after the first day – maybe 300,000
years – the matter and energy became
atoms, then molecules. The physics, having
hooked up with the chemistry, a little while
later – give or take a few billion years –
along came biology when molecules formed
structures called organisms and those, like
us, began making structures called cultures.

In time – by now everything is in time –
human culture produced history. Although
it was her story too. And the earliest of the
stories were stories of faith.

Stories in which people, warming
themselves around a fire and gazing into
endless night sky, recalled the original
cracking of a cosmic egg which gave birth to
everything; or how heroic figures travelled
through fantastical distant realms to reach
this one; or how a supernatural bird sent
from on high dived into the primordial sea
to retrieve the mud which became our earth;
or how the all-powerful creator invented
everything out of nothing in six days and
– this being a major undertaking and quite
tiring – decided that a short lie down was in
order.

People have always asked: 'Where did we
come from and how? The stories are how
we told each other about our place in the
cosmological order. How we told each other
– in painting and music, in poetry and song
– that our lives have meaning. We updated
the stories as our knowledge developed, as
science disclosed the hidden laws that make
life possible, as technology enabled us to
thrive, not just survive.

For a long time, faith and science lived
happily in the stories, but eventually the
gatekeepers of faith became insecure about
the encroachment of science, the rise of
which began to suggest the fall of faith. And
the scientists became evangelical.

The biologist Richard Dawkins says: 'Faith is
the great cop-out, the great excuse to evade
the need to think and evaluate evidence.'[2]
Others scientists, like Albert Einstein, said
we needed both: 'Science without religion
is lame; religion without science is blind.'[3]
The evolutionary biologist Stephen Jay
Gould saw science and religion as two
kinds of 'nets': 'Science tries to document
the factual character of the natural world,
and to develop theories that coordinate and
explain these facts. Religion, on the other
hand, operates in the equally important, but
utterly different, realm of human purposes,
meanings, and values – subjects that the
factual domain of science might illuminate,
but can never resolve.'[4]

In the quest for the truth about how and
why there is something rather than nothing,
people began to understand that maybe
science and faith are fellow travellers. They
come up with different answers because
they ask different questions.

Rabbi Jonathan Sacks puts it this way:
'Science is about explanation. Religion is
about meaning. Science analyses, religion
integrates. Science breaks things down to
their component parts. Religion binds people
together in relationships of trust. Science
tells us what is. Religion tells us what ought
to be. Science describes. Religion beckons,
summons, calls. Science sees objects.

'Religion speaks to us as subjects. Science
practices detachment. Religion is the art of
attachment, self to self, soul to soul. Science
sees the underlying order of the physical
world. Religion hears the music beneath the
noise. Science is the conquest of ignorance.
Religion is the redemption of solitude.'[5]

50

Only remember

Fading away like the stars of the morning
Losing their light in the glorious sun
Thus would we pass from the earth and
its toiling,
Only remembered by what we have done...[1]

So runs the nineteenth-century hymn 'Only Remembered' by Horatius Bonar.

Every headstone tells a story. A soldier who lost his life in the Great War. A baby buried at three weeks old in the 1850s. A policeman who died 'bravely doing his duty'. The mossy headstones in many an urban graveyard, or village burial ground, are like antique tweets, concise tablets of memory, keeping alive the narrative of history behind bramble and branches. They tell us if war was underway, or an epidemic in full force. If there was civil unrest. How the times were a-changing.

Adjust your vision from the dog walkers having a smoke on a bench, look past the leaf-sodden pathways and find a forgotten history, a place where the dead keep our memories. The act of remembering – in a calendar, or on a headstone – is time well spent.

Autumn offers a season of rememb–ering, which once had its own chant. *'Remember, remember, the fifth of November...'*. The surface memory may obscure a deeper, more troubling one. If this English folk verse originated in the failure of the Catholic Guy Fawkes's attempt to blow up the Protestant-run Houses of Parliament in 1605, its apparent anti-treason message was often cover for anti-Catholic prejudice. But Bonfire Night has been the victim of a reverse takeover by Halloween – and the meaning of Halloween has changed too. It was not always about opening the door to seven-year-olds in fright masks. In the Christian tradition, it begins three days of Hallowmas: All Hallows' Eve (Halloween) followed by All Hallows' Day or All Saints' Day, which is followed by All Souls' Day. The dead are remembered. In some countries they call it the Day of the Dead.

In the same season, on 11 November, at war memorials around the country people stop still and stand silent on Remembrance Day. The silence speaks sadness but also protest at the way things are. Somewhere underneath, it may also speak of a longing for a different future. Summoning the past into the present we try to remember another future.

A conversation with a First World War veteran who'd worked with horses gave novelist Michael Morpurgo an idea for a story about Joey, a horse purchased by the Army to serve in the war and how Albert, his previous owner, tried to bring him home.

In the long-running stage play of *War Horse*, one song haunts the imagination: 'Only Remembered' is adapted from Horatius Bonar's hymn. The original text – in which the faithful believer is rewarded in heaven – can't make the transition to a play about the horror of the Great War. But there is a common truth: that what we do here and now is how we will be remembered. That who we are now is who we become in the future. The song remembers the past, but also asks how what we do now will make a difference to those in the future, when we too are the past:

Only the truth that in life we have spoken,
Only the seed that on earth we have sown;
These shall pass onward when we are
forgotten.[2]

LA BOISSELLE, THE SOMME

51

Show compassion

What if we could identify a single principle at the heart of the religious instinct, one that all the great faith traditions agree on? When the philosopher and historian Karen Armstrong asked herself this question, she realised it came down to one word: compassion.

All faiths insist that compassion is the test of true spirituality and that it brings us into relation with the transcendence we call God, Brahman, Nirvana, or Dao. Each has formulated its own version of what is sometimes called the golden rule: 'Do not treat others as you would not like them to treat you,' or in its positive form: 'Always treat others as you would wish to be treated yourself.' Further, they all insist that you cannot confine your benevolence to your own group; you must have concern for everybody – even your enemies.[1]

After Armstrong received the $100,000 TED Prize in 2008, she embarked on a campaign to develop a 'Charter for Compassion, crafted by a group of leading inspirational thinkers, and based on the fundamental principles of universal justice and respect.'

Over eighteen months, 150,000 people submitted suggestions, and in 2009 the Charter for Compassion was unveiled. 'Compassion does not mean pity,' says Armstrong. 'It means to "experience with" the other. The golden rule, of always treating all others as you would wish to be treated yourself, lies at the heart of all morality. It requires a principled, ethical and imaginative effort to put self-interest to one side and stand in somebody else's shoes.'[2]

THE CHARTER FOR COMPASSION

The principle of compassion lies at the heart of all religious, ethical and spiritual traditions, calling us always to treat all others as we wish to be treated ourselves. Compassion impels us to work tirelessly to alleviate the suffering of our fellow creatures, to dethrone ourselves from the centre of our world and put another there, and to honour the inviolable sanctity of every single human being, treating everybody, without exception, with absolute justice, equity and respect.

It is also necessary in both public and private life to refrain consistently and empathically from inflicting pain. To act or speak violently out of spite, chauvinism, or self-interest, to impoverish, exploit or deny basic rights to anybody, and to incite hatred by denigrating others – even our enemies – is a denial of our common humanity. We acknowledge that we have failed to live compassionately and that some have even increased the sum of human misery in the name of religion.

We therefore call upon all men and women to restore compassion to the centre of morality and religion – to return to the ancient principle that any interpretation of scripture that breeds violence, hatred or disdain is illegitimate – to ensure that youth are given accurate and respectful information about other traditions, religions and cultures – to encourage a positive appreciation of cultural and religious diversity – to cultivate an informed empathy with the suffering of all human beings – even those regarded as enemies.

We urgently need to make compassion a clear, luminous and dynamic force in our polarised world. Rooted in a principled determination to transcend selfishness, compassion can break down political, dogmatic, ideological and religious boundaries. Born of our deep interdependence, compassion is essential to human relationships and to a fulfilled humanity. It is the path to enlightenment, and indispensable to the creation of a just economy and a peaceful global community.[3]

52

Unplug yourself

On their 2000 album *Kid A*, the band Radiohead recorded a song called 'How to Disappear Completely'.[1] In 2016, they tried to do just that. Their website faded to blank. Facebook and Twitter feeds were erased, leaving only a mysterious Instagram clip: a clay model of a chirping blackbird.

This sudden absence turned out to be a clever marketing ruse. The blackbird featured in a video for a new song and Radiohead's absence was designed only to underline their presence. You can only reappear if you've disappeared.

In an era where nearly half of us are online, where people keep their smartphones by their beds, disappearing is more difficult than it once was. It's harder to get away when we're all wired up to each other. Some days all our links feel like a chain. When he was asked why he wasn't on email, the late Irish writer, John O'Donohue, replied that he didn't want to return from a walk in the hills and find seventy people waiting for him in the kitchen. Later on he gave in, and his kitchen was soon heaving like everyone else's.

Once, we could easily disappear into a good book, but now, a smartphone looks longingly at us, begging to be held, and can break the spell of the story we're in. When a teenager fails to return a text her parents fear the worst – forgetting that such instant connection didn't exist when they were kids themselves. Forgetting a time when they might have disappeared for hours before anyone became concerned.

But deciding to make our own periodic and temporary disappearances can be transformative. In the same way that a good sleep invites the mind to untangle a knot of thoughts, so the act of disconnection can spark better connections. 'Almost everything will work again if you unplug it for a few minutes,' says Anne Lamott. 'Including you.[2]'

As Jesus of Nazareth said on one of his own periodic disappearing days, 'Come apart to a deserted place by yourself and rest.' Which, being translated, means: 'Log off.'

Tell your phone it's nothing personal as you pop it in a drawer. Go for a wander with no destination in mind. Vanish into the diary you wanted to write. Push open the door of an empty, silent church.

Disconnect, and disappear yourself. Just for an hour or two.

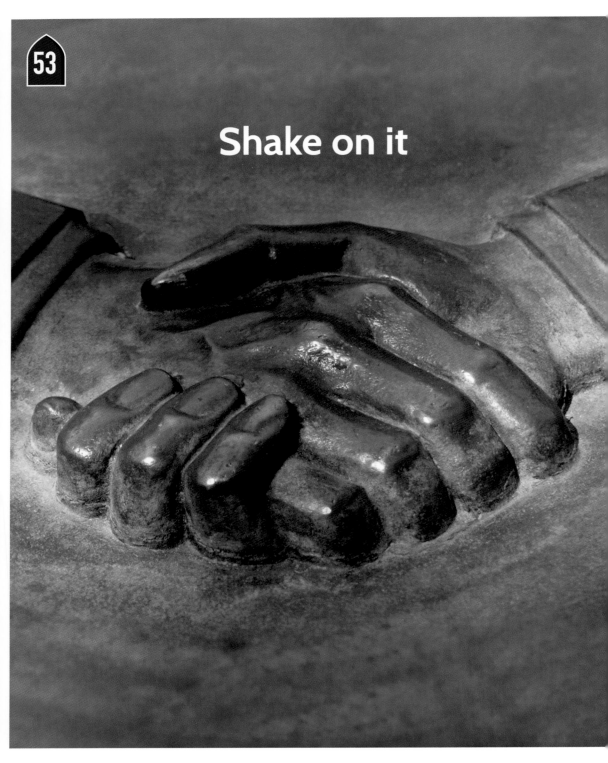

53

Shake on it

SHAKING HANDS

Because what's the alternative?
Because of courage.
Because of loved ones lost.
Because no more.
Because it's a small thing; shaking hands; it happens
every day.
Because I heard of one man whose hands haven't
stopped shaking since a market day in Omagh.
Because it takes a second to say hate, but it takes
longer, much longer, to be a great leader.
Much, much longer.

Because shared space without human touching
doesn't amount to much.
Because it's easier to speak to your own than to
hold the hand of someone whose side has been
previously described, proscribed, denied.
Because it is tough.
Because it is tough.
Because it is meant to be tough, and this is the stuff
of memory, the stuff of hope, the stuff of gesture,
and meaning and leading.
Because it has taken so, so long.
Because it has taken land and money and languages
and barrels and barrels of blood and grieving.
Because lives have been lost.
Because lives have been taken.

Because to be bereaved is to be troubled by grief.
Because more than two troubled peoples live here.
Because I know a woman whose hand hasn't been
shaken since she was a man.
Because shaking a hand is only a part of the start.
Because I know a woman whose touch calmed a
man whose heart was breaking.
Because privilege is not to be taken lightly.

Because this just might be good.
Because who said that this would be easy?
Because some people love what you stand for, and
for some, if you can, they can.
Because solidarity means a common hand.
Because a hand is only a hand; so hang onto it.

So join your much discussed hands.
We need this; for one small second.
So touch.
So lead.[1]

PÁDRAIG Ó TUAMA

This poem was written to mark the occasion in 2012, when the Queen and Martin McGuinness, Sinn Féin's deputy first minister shook hands publicly for the first time after decades of sectarian conflict in Northern Ireland.

54

Bear Witness

Our strategy should be not only to confront empire, but to lay siege to it. To deprive it of oxygen. To shame it. To mock it. With our art, our music, our literature, our stubbornness, our joy, our brilliance, our sheer relentlessness – and our ability to tell our own stories. Stories that are different from the ones we're being brainwashed to believe. The corporate revolution will collapse if we refuse to buy what they are selling – their ideas, their version of history, their wars, their weapons, their notion of inevitability. Remember this: We be many and they be few. They need us more than we need them. Another world is not only possible, she is on her way. On a quiet day, I can hear her breathing.[1]

ARUNDHATI ROY

Does a million people on a march make any difference? Does 2 million?

There are moments in history when we are so incensed at the direction our politicians want to take us, at the laws they want to enact, that all we can do is take to the streets. Or when national leaders act only for national interest, when the challenges of our shared planet can only be faced with global collaboration.

Even the politically shy and retiring find their patience stretched, decide that their only course of action is holding high a handwritten slogan in the company of fellow discontents. 'I am no longer accepting the things I cannot change,' as one banner had it after the 2017 US presidential inauguration. 'I am changing the things I cannot accept.'

But how come so many people seem to be protesting the same things after so many years of protesting those things? Climate change, institutional racism, LGBT+ rights, gender equality, anti-capitalism. Critics claim demonstrations are incoherent and naive. Against the patriarchy, in favour of rainbows; against tanks, in favour of flowers. But the patriarchy is resilient. Like racism and homophobia, like hatred of Jews or hatred of Muslims. As one placard put it in 2017: 'I can't believe I still have to protest this fucking shit.' The sentiment was borrowed from a young black woman protesting racism in 2014, half a century after the dawn of the Civil Rights movement. Occasionally a great uprising of people power ignites dramatic political change – like the fall of the Berlin Wall. More likely, say the cynics, mass protest movements are just virtue-signalling, a way of saying to like-minded people that you're on their team. When, they ask, did the Occupy movement achieve the reform of capitalism?

But viewing the efficacy of mass protest in short-term policy shifts is not the only lens to use. Asked how he wished to be remembered, the neurologist Oliver Sacks said he'd like it to be thought, 'that I had listened carefully to what patients and others have told me'. To use a biblical term, he added, he'd like it to be thought that he 'bore witness'.[2]

Sacks understood the significance of bearing witness to the lives of others, often those ostracised or ignored. The most powerful uprisings of public disquiet or longing for social change, are not those which are simply about standing up for people but those which are about standing alongside people. Standing with people when the march is over, people where we live or work.

Elie Wiesel lost his sister and mother in Auschwitz, and his father at Buchenwald. His novel *Night* is about his first night in a camp, 'those moments that murdered my God and my soul and turned my dreams to ashes for ever'. Wiesel spent much of the rest of his life with Holocaust survivors and came to see his role as that of 'a witness', to guard against history repeating itself: 'To listen to a witness is to become a witness and that consoles us.'[3]

How effective is it when we take to the streets in mass protest? 'We may never know what will result of these actions,' said Gandhi, 'but if you do nothing there will be no results.'[4]

In taking action we bear witness not just to the urgent needs of others but to the direction of history itself. We bear witness by telling another kind of story, says the novelist Arundhati Roy, by trying to hear the quiet breath of another kind of world.

55

I AM BECAUSE YOU ARE

'To be is to do' (Socrates)
'To do is to be' (Sartre)
'Do Be Do Be Do' (Sinatra)[1]

This was how novelist Kurt Vonnegut summed up our existential quest to answer the biggest questions. The seventeenth-century French philosopher René Descartes came up with his own pithy aphorism to explain who and why we are: 'I think, therefore I am.'

He didn't make the cut in the Vonnegut joke, but René found himself in another one, in which he walks into a bar and is asked if he'd like a beer. 'I think not,' he replies... and promptly disappears.

Do we live in our heads? Or in our daily actions? Come to think of it, how do we even know we're here? Enlightenment thinkers like Descartes were not just big on reason but also on individualism, an influence that shapes our twenty-first century world of capitalism, commerce and consumption. A world captured in another soundbite: 'I shop, therefore I am.'

Individualism also informs what we talk about when we talk about God. How do I get to heaven? Why do I feel bad about myself? How do I become a better person?

But in Southern Africa a bantu word – *ubuntu* – suggests an alternative way of answering the big questions. Ubuntu can best be translated as 'I am because you are'.[2] It's a word that signals how each of us finds our best self only in relationship to others. How life is not to be understood as a solitary, individual pursuit but as something we share. That we understand ourselves better when we live in company not alone. 'Ubuntu speaks about the fact that you can't exist as a human being in isolation,' says Archbishop Desmond Tutu: 'It speaks about our interconnectedness. You can't be human all by yourself... we think of ourselves frequently as just individuals, separated from one another, whereas we are connected and what we do affects the whole world.'[3]

This is counter-intuitive in a culture where our goals often centre on personal fulfilment – in family or career. In spirituality and religion. But many of our deepest questions can't be answered in isolation, only in friendship. Many of them – 'why is there so much suffering?' – can barely be answered at all. We have to live with these questions. But living with them with others sometimes means we become the answers ourselves.

Those others might be a lonely neighbour, an annoying relative, a sick child, an estranged partner. Or they might be losing hope in Syria, locked up in Guantánamo, forgotten in Gaza. They might be the people we meet when we hesitatingly volunteer at that rough sleepers' hostel – or step over the threshold of a local synagogue, mosque, or church.

Religion is not a solitary business, it's a communal one. Do it on your own and you'll probably give up – watching all these strange beliefs and practices slipping through your fingers like sand. But one of the virtues in being part of a faith community is that on the days when you are mainly full of doubt, someone else can do the believing on your behalf.

And there might even be the odd day, when you find you're the one with enough faith for two, a day when someone else has none. It's not about you. It's about us. To be is to be together. 'I am because you are.'

56

Fail Again.
Fail Better.

In 1993, when the Dual Cyclone vacuum cleaner arrived, people praised the genius of inventor James Dyson. The same James Dyson who had been less celebrated in the previous fifteen years when he had come up with 5,126 machines, before the one that worked. 'But I learned from each one,' he said. 'That's how I came up with a solution. So I don't mind failure.'[1]

Dyson's failures quietly made him.

Failure gets a bad press. Considering that it's endured by anyone who is successful, that it's the only route to success. Witness the business ideas that didn't take off... before the one that did. The rejection letters to (later) famous authors. The fabled gigs with seven in the audience of (later) bestselling bands.

The path of failure can also lead to the success we weren't seeking. When you're next spraying lubricant on a creaking door hinge, take a moment to give thanks to Dr Norm Larsen of the Rocket Chemical Company. Norm was not thinking door hinges. His thoughts were about creating a formula to stop corrosion in nuclear missiles. But Norm failed. Then Norm failed again. Norm failed thirty-nine times until finally his snappily titled 'Water Displacement' product came good at the fortieth attempt. But no one thinks less of Norm's WD-40 because WD-1 to WD-39 were failures.

And our mistakes may tell us more than our successes even though, at the time, defeat is hard to accept. Who wants to feel like a failure? But dashed hopes, thwarted plans or mistaken calculations can be paradoxically illuminating. A counter-intuitive thought in a note from the biblical letter-writer Paul puts it like this: 'Power is made perfect in weakness.'[2]

The story of scientific understanding is one of blind alleys and failed experiments, of reversing up dead-end streets to think again. 'The entire scientific method,' says astrophysicist Mario Livi, 'is based on the notion that discovering what does *not* work is vital to learning what does.'[3]

Every day is trial and error, which is how, when we reflect, we come to understand ourselves and learn to relate to each other.

'I've always thought that schoolchildren should be marked by the number of failures they've had,' says James Dyson. 'The child who tries strange things and experiences lots of failures to get there is probably more creative.'[4]

'Make interesting mistakes,' the writer Neil Gaiman told a class of graduating students. 'Make amazing mistakes, make glorious and fantastic mistakes. Break rules. Leave the world more interesting for your being here.'[5]

Every hesitant folly or bold failure helps us refine the experiment we call our life. 'Ever tried. Ever failed,' asked Samuel Beckett. 'No matter. Try Again. Fail again. Fail better.'[6]

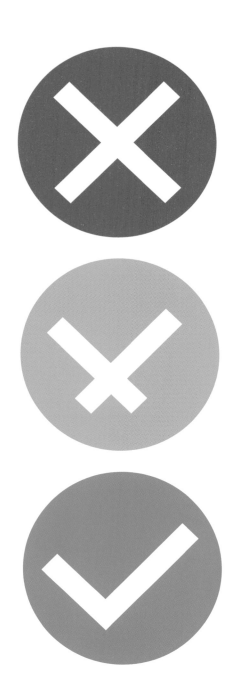

57

SEX IT UP

'Between consenting adults, in private.' It's the sexual norm for almost every society on earth, and the legal definition in most countries.

It's not the most poetic phrase but, to be fair, it's there for legal clarification, and for essential personal protection. And very reasonable. Trouble is, sex itself is not reasonable at all. It's primal. It's sensual, lustful, passionate and sticky. The cognitive scientist and psychologist Steven Pinker says: 'Sex and excretion are reminders that anyone's claim to round-the-clock dignity is tenuous. The so-called rational animal has a desperate drive to pair up and moan and writhe.'[1] The songwriter Bruce Cockburn captures it:

When two lovers really love there's nothing there

But this suddenly compact universe
Of skin and breath and hair.[2]

If there's a moment when we as humans really let go, it's in the instant of sexual climax. Pure pleasure – ecstasy. Heaven. That's why religion often tries to put the dampener on it. And because sex is such a visceral drive, to the degree that our bodies can easily rule our heads, and hearts – it's readily exploited, commodified. People with influence, or glamour, or money, or guns, can use sex to express their power. Meanwhile, people without those advantages are driven to sell their bodies to gratify the appetite of others.

For animals, sex is mostly about procreation – though researchers suggest

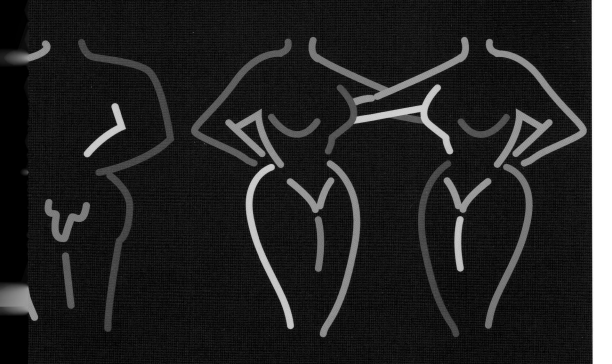

that, in some species, this may not entirely be the case. And while making babies is hugely enjoyable for humans, it's about a whole lot more. The powerful urge is still there, but it's not simply a question of satisfying a physical hunger.

It's about coupling – in the most generous sense of the word. It's equally shared touch, heat, smell. Profound intimacy. It's an eloquence of trust and fidelity. Our bodies tell each other what we love about them.

Sacred texts are often taken to assume that this takes place between one gender and another. The creation myth of the Hebrew and Christian scriptures, for instance, talks of the joint creation of man and woman, saying: 'Therefore shall a man leave his father and his mother, and shall cleave unto his wife and they shall be one flesh.' Great word, 'cleave'. This, of course, was written before there was much understanding of the fluidity of gender and orientation. But it's the underlying wisdom that counts. It's the *cleaving* that matters, however we're built. The seventeenth-century King James Bible says that when we have sex with someone, we 'know' them.

'Real intimacy is a sacred experience,' says the poet John O'Donohue. 'It never exposes its secret trust and belonging to the voyeuristic eye of a neon culture. Real intimacy is of the soul, and the soul is reserved.'[3]

Body and soul, consenting, in private.

58

Live with
the unknown

'All will be revealed!' – the promise of the final episode of the TV thriller – 'Tune in next week and find out who did what and when.'

Revelations are the meat and drink of the media. *He's* been seen leaving a party with *her*. *She's* broken up with *him*. *They're* having a baby, buying a puppy, or going on holiday. We're given the inside track on love affairs, financial deals and political dramas. We're offered the answers to the questions everyone is said to be asking.

But do we get the whole story? Often facts are few and far between, and wrapped up in speculation. And we also know that when we talk to friends who've experienced a falling out at work or in a relationship we're only getting one side of the story. The worlds of life and love, faith and doubt are messy.

It's hard to be sure of the absolute truth about anything. Hardly a day goes by without new research that wine or coffee or chocolate is good for us... when last year we were told the opposite.

Even scientific giants such as Sir Isaac Newton, who reckoned the world ran a bit like clockwork, are called into question, as quantum physicists scratch their heads over the uncertain behaviour of sub-atomic particles. We have to admit to a certain fuzziness about how things are. Truth is usually provisional.

Religions have a tendency to claim that their understanding of existence is the unassailable truth. They will assert that their sacred texts are not so much human documents as direct divine revelations. Sometimes the authors of these works seem to have lived special lives, better and more selfless than most of us. But it's still difficult to see them as the flawless repository of truth for all time.

If we're lucky we sometimes grasp moments of truth, sense we've understood something previously obscure. We feel, for a moment, enlightened – about each other, about our world, about this life. But, as the apostle Paul wrote, a lot of the time we 'see through a glass, darkly'. All has *not* been revealed. The theologian Barbara Brown Taylor writes: 'New life starts in the dark. Whether it is a seed in the ground, a baby in the womb, or Jesus in the tomb, it starts in the dark.'[1]

We don't have all the facts. And we never will. That's not to say that ignorance is bliss, or that we should stifle our curiosity. Just that it's okay to be agnostic. To live with the unknown. Even to welcome it.

59

Say a little prayer

It's true that prayer is something practised by people of faith, that prayer is 'religious'. But it's also true that the impulse to pray goes back further than organised religion, that it's a human instinct. The desire to seek help in a time of trouble or give thanks when life is good.

And if certain kinds of prayer look for a divine connection –

**Operator
Information
Give me Jesus on the line**[1]

– not all prayer does.

Uttering a prayer can also act as a note to self. Just as writers will say that writing something down helps them understand what they think, so people in therapy will say that expressing their feelings in a safe environment gives them a new way of understanding themselves. Saying a prayer – writing it down, speaking it out – can do something similar. Bring us clarity, help us reconsider, offer us resolution.

And the Old English word 'Amen' – the full stop at the end of many prayers – is the act of affirmation that says: 'make it so'.

**Write your own prayers.
Speak them out.**

Make it so.

This one's for you, sitting opposite me. Whatever it is you need, I hope you get it. (And let's hope that someone, today, will send one out for me.) **Amen.**

For that last breath. And this next one. For this heart, which keeps on beating even though I never notice. For being here. For being alive. Thanks. **Amen.**

I wonder where she's from. Originally. The life she left behind. I couldn't be doing what she's doing, unless I was desperate. God help her. **Amen.**

I can't stand this job. There, I've said it. I need to change something. I need to make a new start. Maybe today. So. Help. Me. **Amen.**

I shouldn't have said that. Something snapped. I lost it. I sometimes do. He was wrong. But all the same, so was I. Sorry about that. I mean it. **Amen.**

This is me wishing things were different. Wishing the world well. Wishing you well. Today. Saying a prayer. **Amen**.

I'm not going to let this wind me up. Someone, somewhere is facing something far more serious. God help them. (And me too while you're at it.) **Amen.**

Thanks for her. And for him. For her wise words and his kind smile. Thank you people. You know who you are. **Amen.**

60

IT IS SOLVED B

Life is sometimes compared to a journey. Quite often actually. At decisive moments we see ourselves at a 'crossroads'. We talk of 'the onward march of history' to reflect a longer route trod by the whole human race, underway long before we showed up, continuing after we've left.

Make this journey as part of a faith community, and sometimes we recall being given a map. Sitting down at our metaphorical roadside, we unpack our sandwiches and flask of tea and spread out this map. Unfortunately, as the poet Stephen Levine put it, while Buddha, Jesus and Krishna each left maps of a kind, 'you still have to travel the road yourself'.[1]

Folds and creases obscure the cartography, the map is a little too open to interpretation. In low moments we might hum a little tune by Talking Heads, 'The Road to Nowhere'.[2] How did we get here anyway, and what are we looking for?

Some people have a clear destination in mind, and a short-cut to get there. The answer to 'the ultimate question of life, the universe and everything is 42' wrote Douglas Adams in *The Hitchhiker's Guide to the Galaxy*.[3] Yes, he's having a laugh, but some people don't get the joke – that there isn't anything as tawdry as an 'answer'. That there is no accurate map and, anyway, the place we're looking for can never be pinpointed. 'It is not down on any map,' Herman Melville put it in *Moby Dick*. 'True places never are.'

But still, the journey.

Since 1865 Hackney carriage and then black cab drivers have been obliged to complete 'the Knowledge', several years training in London's eccentric jigsaw of highways and byways. The few who pass the test develop an encyclopaedic knowledge of the city, more nuanced with every fare. Scientists found these cabbies often have an enlarged hippocampus, the area of the brain

WALKING *(solvitur ambulando)*

associated in animals with navigation. And then satnav arrived – putting the cabbie on the endangered species list.

But if information may displace knowledge on our roads, on our metaphorical journey speed is not of the essence; the wisdom of tried and trusted experience will not be overtaken. Sometimes we need to take the scenic route, even if it makes us late.

*... Life is not hurrying
on to a receding future, nor hankering after
an imagined past*[4]

wrote the poet R. S. Thomas. Instead it's stopping to notice – and cherish – these days we have now. For this we need wise travelling companions, people who've been this way before. If we can see past their frailty or failing memory, we will notice such guides – let's call them old people – all around. They made their mistakes but also, sometimes learnt from them.

To our information society they bring wisdom which is why, in many cultures, they are not dismissed as 'past their sell by' but revered as elders. 'Grey hair,' reads the Bible, 'is a crown of glory, Wisdom is with the aged.' Do not forsake wisdom, it adds, 'she will protect you; love her, and she will watch over you'.

If we learn from experience that there is no 'answer' to life, no direct route to our destination, we may also discover that the concept of truth will not be reduced to information or mathematical formula. That a film or a poem can also be true, a friend can be true, even a way of life. 'To believe in God' said Ludwig Wittgenstein, 'is to know that the facts of the world are not the end of the matter.'[5]

We take most of our questions along with us on the way and we make the way by walking. A Latin phrase is as good a motto for the journey as any – *solvitur ambulando* – it is solved by walking.

From the meaning of life to the problem of pain, from our broken relationships to our longing for love, answers are few and far between. Some days we just keep on keeping on, and some days it is solved by walking.

'NEVER FORGET THAT JUSTICE IS

T **LOVE** LOOKS LIKE IN PUBLIC'

CORNEL WEST[1]

Question everything

What advice on life would an extraterrestrial offer us? An alien working out how to adjust to a strange humanoid reality, arriving from some distant galaxy? After a brief experimental period, what would this visitor from another planet conclude about what constitutes a good life?

That's the essence of Matt Haig's novel *The Humans*,[1] in which a visitor from Vonnadoria – where life revolves around maths, logic and rationality – tries to sum up the essence of a rewarding life on planet earth. He distills his newfound wisdom into a list of ninety-four items entitled 'Advice for A Human'. Here are some of the best:

Don't worry about your abilities. You have the ability to love. That is enough...

Be curious. Question everything. A present fact is just a future fiction...

You shouldn't have been born. Your existence is as close to impossible as can be. To dismiss the impossible is to dismiss yourself...

Your life will have 30,000 days in it. Make sure you remember some of them...

If there is a sunset, stop and look at it. Knowledge is finite. Wonder is infinite...

One day humans will live on Mars. But nothing there will be more exciting than a single overcast morning on Earth...

Don't always try and be cool. The whole universe is cool. It's the warm bits that matter...

You have the power to stop time. You do it by kissing. Or listening to music...

Don't ever be afraid of telling someone you love them. There are things wrong with your world, but an excess of love is not one...

Politeness is often fear. Kindness is always courage. But caring is what makes you human. Care more, become more human...

You can't find happiness looking for the meaning of life. Meaning is only the third most important thing. It comes after loving and being...

VONNADORIA, 9 MILLION LIGHT YEARS FROM EARTH

63

Take a day off

Next time someone asks you 'What has religion ever done for us?' try these on them:

Wesak
Diwali
Eid al-Fitr
Pesach
Christmas
Parinirvana Day
Holi
Hanukkah
Easter
Eid al-Adha

There are more. Hinduism has more than a thousand. What are they? Holy days, from which we get our more common 'holiday'. And to which we might add less sacred versions, including Duvet Day and the Throwing of the Sickie Day.

Everyone needs a day off. According to *Genesis*, the first book in the Bible, even God needed a lie down after slogging away all week in creating the cosmos. 'And he rested on the seventh day from all his work which he had made.' Out of this grew traditions in the Abrahamic faiths – Judaism, Islam, Christianity – about setting aside a weekly 'sabbath', a day of rest.

And while religious holy days may be notionally focused on founders' birthdays and lunar and seasonal cycles, at grassroots level they're basically an excuse for some well-earned R & R. The busier our days become, the more essential it is to set aside rest days. 'We humans have lost the wisdom of genuinely resting and relaxing,' says Buddhist monk Thich Nhat Hanh. 'We worry too much. We don't allow our bodies to heal, and we don't allow our minds and hearts to heal.'[1]

Often the ancient traditions of good religion are reminders of how to live a good life. Like nature, rest is vital for regeneration. 'Take rest,' said the Roman poet Ovid. 'A field that has rested gives a more beautiful crop.'[2]

'Each person deserves a day away in which no problems are confronted, no solutions searched for. Each of us needs to withdraw from the cares which will not withdraw from us,'[3] wrote Maya Angelou.

Why not take the rest of the day off?

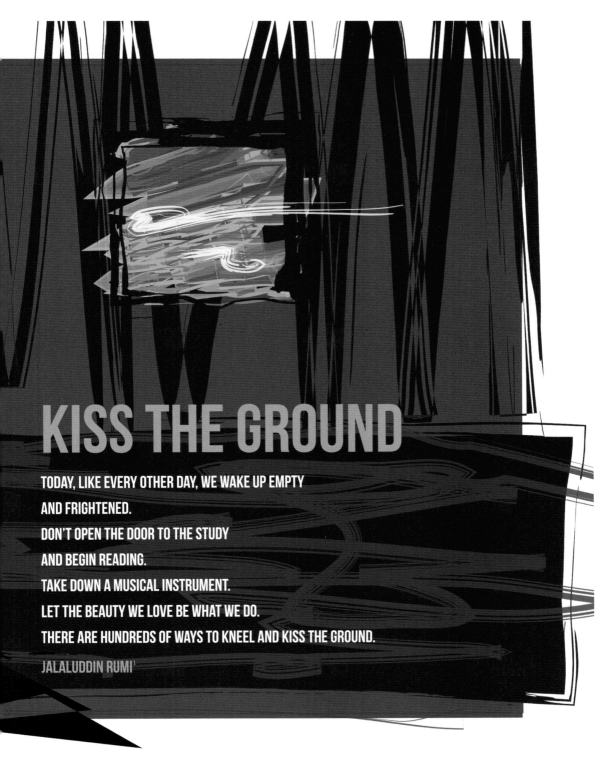

KISS THE GROUND

TODAY, LIKE EVERY OTHER DAY, WE WAKE UP EMPTY

AND FRIGHTENED.

DON'T OPEN THE DOOR TO THE STUDY

AND BEGIN READING.

TAKE DOWN A MUSICAL INSTRUMENT.

LET THE BEAUTY WE LOVE BE WHAT WE DO.

THERE ARE HUNDREDS OF WAYS TO KNEEL AND KISS THE GROUND.

JALALUDDIN RUMI[1]

Find your
own way
home

'Exile is more than a geographical concept,' said Mahmoud Darwish. 'You can be an exile in your homeland, in your own house, in a room.'[1]

He, himself, was no stranger to exile. The Palestinian, Muslim poet first had to leave home in 1948, aged seven, when the Israeli army attacked his village in western Galilee. He was exiled again for twenty years between the 1970s and 1990s, and even when he later settled in the West Bank town of Ramallah, he never felt at home.

Many people, like Darwish, are driven into exile in foreign lands, for reasons of politics, persecution or conflict. They accommodate to their new surroundings, but at heart there remains a painful sense of homelessness. For some exiled communities this is expressed in a nostalgia for language, food, objects, traditions, which provide comfort and bolster their sense of identity.

But, as Darwish says, exile can be as much a matter of the mind or spirit as about physical location. In the UK, some of those who voted to leave the European Union in the 2016 referendum claimed they felt alienated from their own country, because they felt their sovereignty had been hijacked or because of the influx of immigrants. But large numbers of those who had voted to remain, protested that – following the result – they themselves felt their country had been stolen from them under false pretences.

Minorities – for example, people with disabilities, individuals in the LGBT+ community, people of colour – often feel marginalised and disadvantaged. Alienated. We are increasingly strangers to the land itself. 'We try to exile ourselves more and more from nature – not always consciously,' says the American naturalist Diane Ackerman: 'We build houses; we dismiss nature; nature has to be outside, because we're inside. God forbid something like a cockroach comes inside, or some dust.'[2]

But exile need not necessarily be terminal. At the turn of the fourth and fifth century BC, Nebuchadnezzar destroyed Jerusalem, and condemned almost all Israelites to exile in Babylon. Dark days. They had thought they had a divine guarantee of protection and prosperity. But exile wasn't the end, observed the scholar Walter Brueggemann: 'Exile did not lead Jews in the Old Testament to abandon faith or to settle for abdicating despair, nor to retreat to privatistic religion. On the contrary, exile evoked the most brilliant literature and the most daring theological articulation in the Old Testament. It was during the exile that they gathered their scriptures, their traditions and culture around them. And dared to hope.'[3]

Mahmoud Darwish responded in a similar way to his exile: 'I've built my homeland, I've even founded my own state – in my language.' And, as exiles across history and around the world have done, he held on, planned a return home. 'We suffer from an incurable malady,' he said: 'Hope.'[4]

The Jewish philosopher Martin Buber said: 'Everyone must come out of his own Exile in his own way.'[5] Whenever, however, we're exiled, we need to find our way home.

66

It's a story as old as the hills. The hills being those in the original creation story of the great Abrahamic faiths, the hills being conjured up by the Maker of All Things. In the shake of a figleaf, the serpent tempted Eve – the suggestible, flaky female type in the original patriarchal worldview – who ate the apple and offered it to Adam.

Adam also took a bite, at which point both realised they had no clothes on, were overcome with shame... and the age of innocence was at an end.

If the story captures deep stuff about misogyny, body image and... snakes, it's also deep on something religions have majored on ever since. Sin.

Sin is the most popular religious explanation for our existential angst, the separation of creature from creator. It was in this Eden that we originally fell into sin. 'We acknowledge and bewail our manifold sins and wickedness,' as it's put in the Book of Common Prayer of the Church of England. 'There is no health in us miserable offenders.'

Cast out of Paradise and cut off from our divine home, different faith traditions offer competing routes of return. But the lexicon of sin, wickedness and moral depravity is less persuasive than it once was. One problem, says novelist Francis Spufford, is that sin has been redefined as 'the pleasurable consumption of something',[1] and usually connected to sex and/or hatred of the body. The trouble is that sin is a word that usefully describes a true human emotion, a notion that still rings true. Most of us feel that we mess up. We fail by our own standards, even if we don't believe there are divine standards.

The human species, says Spufford, suffers from 'HPtFtU' – the 'Human Propensity to Fuck things Up': 'what we're talking about here is not just our tendency to lurch and stumble and screw up by accident, our passive role as agents of entropy. It's our active inclination to break stuff – "stuff" here including moods, promises, relationships we care about and our own wellbeing and other people's, as well as material objects whose high gloss positively seems to invite a big fat scratch.'[2]

That seventeenth-century Prayer Book still touches a nerve when it says we have 'erred, and strayed like lost sheep', or 'followed too much the devices and desires of our own hearts'. Most of us have deliberately been unkind to people, hurt them; been greedy, selfish and proud. It happens. Not just as individuals, but in our families, in our communities, in our countries.

We have fucked up history.

We fail each other. We fail ourselves.

It's part of the truth about ourselves.

And on a good day, we see it. We admit it.

And it's only when we recognise that we fuck things up, and that we're likely to do it again, that we have a chance to do something about it.

When you fail
come clean

67

Be
enchanted

You…

Smell the sea.

Are caught by a familiar song coming from the radio.

Feel a hand squeeze your shoulder.

Lie still, looking up, under a great night sky.

See that person you love approaching.

And what you experience, in that moment, is something more than that which your senses capture. The intensity is deeper than you expect. You sense a connectedness, a gratitude, a wonder. You feel that this is more real than real.

It might only last seconds. Minutes with luck. But it is profound.

Buddhists call feelings like this 'suchness'. Mircea Eliade, a scholar of comparative religions, called them experiences 'of the golden world'.[1] Theologian Marcus Borg talked of being 'filled with glory'.[2]

Everything melts into the present. In his *Varieties of Religious Experience*, psychologist and philosopher William James described a personal instance when: 'The perfect stillness of the night was thrilled by a more solemn silence. The darkness held a presence that was all the more felt because it was not seen.'[3]

Sometimes we get the sense that there is simply *more*. And this more has become known as the 'numinous'.

An experience of the numinous doesn't prove anything, but it does encourage us to embrace sensations which provide a feeling of being whole, and give us a clue that there may be something beyond.

A moment like this is precious, said William James, and something worth holding on to: 'Like love, like wrath, like hope, ambition, jealousy, like every other instinctive eagerness and impulse, it adds to life an enchantment which is not rationally or logically deducible from anything else…'[4]

SOME KEEP THE SABBATH GOING TO CHURCH

Some keep the Sabbath going to Church –
I keep it, staying at Home –
With a Bobolink for a Chorister –
And an Orchard, for a Dome –

Some keep the Sabbath in Surplice –
I just wear my Wings –
And instead of tolling the Bell, for Church,
Our little Sexton – sings.

God preaches, a noted Clergyman –
And the sermon is never long,
So instead of getting to Heaven, at last –
I'm going, all along.[5]

EMILY DICKINSON

68

PAY ATTENTION

There are these two young fish swimming along, and they happen to meet an older fish swimming the other way, who nods at them and says, 'Morning, boys, how's the water?' And the two young fish swim on for a bit, and then eventually one of them looks over at the other and goes, 'What the hell is water?'[1]

DAVID FOSTER WALLACE

It is easy to sleepwalk through our days. To not notice what's going on. Our default position, argued novelist David Foster Wallace, is to be centred on ourselves and our own needs. We're worshipping animals, he said, but our reverence is focused not on the mystical, the beyond, but on self-serving deities like money, intellect and power. Gods that 'will eat you alive'. If these are our sources of meaning, we'll never be satisfied and will want more.

True, they kind of work. We've harnessed them to put ourselves at the centre of everything. But, said Wallace, there are other kinds of freedom: 'The really important kind of freedom involves attention, and awareness, and discipline, and effort, and being able truly to care about other people and to sacrifice for them, over and over, in myriad petty little unsexy ways, every day.'[2]

We have to explore the water that we're swimming in. Examine it. Paying attention to each other and to the vividness of the physical surroundings that lie beyond our personal murk. We find dividends by

Whatever we believe about religion or faith, most people think that love is a good place to start from, a good place to head to and a good way to get there.

'All you need is love,'[1] we sing. And we do need it.

Yes. But. What exactly does that mean?

Love is not a thing, you can get, or own. And it's more than a feeling you find described in a pop song or a sensation that mysteriously comes and goes.

Love is a verb. And a verb – as many of us were taught in primary school – is a *doing* word. Love only has real meaning when we demonstrate it. By being loving. Flowers, and chocolates, and declarations of devotion are not bad. But a kindness is better, an act of selflessness which looks for nothing in return. Actions usually speak louder than words.

When Jesus of Nazareth said: 'Love your neighbour as yourself', he wasn't talking about how we might feel about them but about what we might do for them. He told a story about a traveller who stopped at the scene of a mugging, noticed the victim was not from his class or ethnic group and still took time to look after him, get him to hospital and see that he would be cared for. A victim of street violence and a complete stranger. Practical kindness, one human being to another. Love made real, love as a verb. (And a stranger who is really a neighbour.)

The ancient prophets, such as Amos or Hosea, Micah or Isaiah, banged on about how the rich mistreated the poor, about bribery, unpaid labour or political corruption. They knew that love is more than feeling something. That love is doing something.

Loving someone is the most important thing we can do. Ever. St Paul, who was a serious whinge bag on some days, could also find himself taken with moments of transcendent, poetic insight. In one of his most lyrical moments he compresses all life's virtues down to three: faith, hope... and love, which, he says, is the greatest.

We love someone when we put them at the head of the queue, and ourselves at the back. That's what love does. And we show love, not to make us look good, but because that's what it's all about. Love. Actually.

Come to Jesus

There's a lot about Jesus that would be useful to know which the Bible doesn't mention. Was he short or tall? Fat or slim? Introvert or extrovert? What did he smell like?

We've got four versions of his life, often known as Gospels: Matthew, Mark, Luke and John. They're not biographies but they drop biographical hints. He came from Nazareth, a village about seventy miles east of the lake of Galilee in the region of Palestine, where it can get quite hot. He ate fish, bread, herbs and lamb. He drank wine. So he probably smelt of sweat, dust, red wine, and a hint of garlic. Except on that day when his friend Mary Magdalene (possibly) tipped a jar of the Indian root spikenard on him at a dinner party. That would have added a leathery, aromatic aroma.

People of faith tend to see Jesus as an icon, not a person. They put 'Lord' before his name and 'Christ' after it, and follow it with phrases like 'King of Kings', or 'Lamb of God'.

In Monty Python's *Life of Brian*, Jesus's – sorry, Brian's – mum tells a crowd of wannabe disciples outside the house: 'He's not the Messiah, he's a very naughty boy.'

There aren't enough stories about his upbringing to know whether he was naughty or not, but on the basis that all children are naughty sometimes, Jesus was no saint. He had brothers: James, Joseph, Judas (not that one) and Simon. He had sisters, one of whom may have been called Salome. Although, while he was alive, none of his siblings 'got him' enough to become followers. At one point, it was family members who 'went out to restrain him, for people were saying: "He

has gone out of his mind."'[1] But that might have been a drunk uncle at a wedding.

Maybe his sense of having a special calling rendered him a bit of an outsider. He could be cranky, severe, demanding, infuriating. But also full of love and compassion; an includer, a champion of the outcast.

Sometimes Jesus of Nazareth looks driven and conflicted, sure of himself one moment, plagued by self-doubt the next. He was capable of elation and despair. He got tired, lonely. Horny too, although we don't know if he was gay or straight.

Traditionally we've been told Jesus came to show us how to be divine, but maybe he came to show us how to be human. To reveal the sacred depths within our humanity. To bring us back from the dead.

Sometimes, from those gospel accounts he sounds like he could be the person who's best left alone until after the first coffee of the morning. If he said he was off to the hills for some quiet, best not to ask to tag along. And when he went off on one, best not to suggest that he 'calm down'.

On the other hand, if you were a small child; if your world seemed to be falling apart; if you were being bullied by the authorities; if you were at death's door; if you wanted to know you were loved. He was your man.

In the end, people seemed to know they could trust him. The earth he walked, the Father he spoke with, the people he loved, it all rubbed off on him. You could smell it a mile off.

72

Make big
decisions
slowly...

...and small
decisions
fast

Is he the one? Can I commit?

If they offer it, should I take it?

I've got to say something, but how shall I put it?

It's a lot of money… is it worth it?

Is that really what I want to do with my life?

Decisions, decisions. They punctuate our every waking hour. Most are so routine we barely notice the choice we're making. Some are so significant they may have a bearing on the career we pursue, or the person we spend our days with.

It's said we make 35,000 decisions every day – over 200 just on food. Most are snap judgements drawing on intuition, experience and simple reasoning: 'No sugar, thanks.' But sometimes, coming to a resolution requires time because the consequences may be life changing: 'I do.'

The Jesuit priest James Martin suggests that before starting to think through a decision we should try to be 'indifferent'.[1] He doesn't mean not giving a damn, but finding a sense of detachment and freedom. Step back from the emotions stirred up by a particular quandary and choose to be impartial.

If we can gain some kind of detachment, then we can imaginatively follow the route of a decision in a certain direction. Or the other. Living with that person, how does that feel? Or deciding to live with them… no longer.

The Jesuits draw on the teachings of the fifteenth-century Christian mystic, Ignatius of Loyola, who said that in making decisions we should look for signs in our feelings of 'consolation', or 'desolation'.

A job opportunity, for example, may mean more money and leaping several rungs up a career ladder. It may be a great choice. But if the thought of it leaves you feeling empty, disappointed with yourself – *desolate* – then maybe this job is not quite who you are. Alternatively, if the prospect leaves you with 'a sense of rightness, of peace' – if it leaves you feeling *consoled* – perhaps it would be a move in the right direction.

In big decisions, Ignatius said it helps if you remind yourself of your ultimate objectives in life – the kind of person you want to become. Or to imagine yourself at the end of your life: what would the late and wise version of yourself think about this decision? Would they intervene on behalf of this person being unfairly bad-mouthed? Would they make this investment of time or money? Would they put up with this troubling situation?

What would your 'best self' do? How would the person that you long to be make this choice?

However reliable our instincts, it's wise not to rush into making big decisions. It's wise to imaginatively practise alternative futures, to try them on for size. It's wise to line up the pros and cons… and then to sleep on them. 'Make big decisions slowly, and small decisions fast,' says God, when he turns up for a chat in the kitchen, in a poem by Anthony Wilson.[2]

It's wise to sit quietly, and listen to your deepest self. Now and again, the decision will be made for you.

73

SOME GRACES

Some hae meat and canna eat,
And some wad eat that want it,
But we hae meat and we can eat,
Sae let the Lord be thankit.[3]
The Selkirk Grace
attributed to Robert Burns

This ritual is one. The food is one.
We who offer the food are one. The
fire of hunger is also one. All action
is one. We who understand this are
one.
A Hindu blessing

For the meal we are about to eat,
for those that made it possible, and
for those with whom we are about
to share it, we are thankful.
A humanist blessing

See the entire universe
in the meal you're about to eat

At one time, when people stopped their daily routine for a meal, they would give thanks. In cultures steeped in Christian history, this was called saying grace. Asking a blessing on the food.

But mealtimes metamorphosed as working patterns changed. Now, we eat on the run, or in front of a screen. Alone, rather than in families. New rituals displace old ones. People may still pause religiously before a meal... to snap a photo of the food and Instagram it.

If the earlier ritual was about connecting with the divine, the new one is connecting with each other. Perhaps the thought of giving thanks is no longer thought, because many of us are no longer formally religious. But also because our relationship with food has changed.

In ancient times we produced our own food, or traded it from a neighbour. As in many developing countries today, most people were smallholders – everyday life rooted in the good earth, the soil producing the food which kept everyone alive. Or didn't. Harvest time was precarious and uncertain, which explains that famous line in that famous prayer: 'Give us this day our daily bread.'

But we have become separated from the ground beneath our feet, from the earth that delivers our food and the people who produce it. By the time we eat our breakfast, said Martin Luther King Jr sixty years ago, we've depended 'on half the world'.[1] The world has been shrinking every day since, and now the local shop may have every country on its shelves.

Our fruit and veg comes polished, shrink-wrapped and protected for travel. We don't see the journey it takes to reach us. We don't see Agnes plucking these pears for us in South Africa, or Mary in St Lucia cropping those bananas, or Blaise in Ghana, sorting these tomatoes. We don't notice and we forget to be grateful.

'Dear God,' as Bart Simpson once put it before a meal, 'we paid for all this stuff ourselves, so thanks for nothing!'[2]

If we take for granted those who produce our food, so we can be complacent about the variety and reliability of our food supply. But giving thanks is good:

To God if you believe in her.

Or to those invisible people in the supply chain who harvested our food.

Or those visible people who produced it, in our kitchen.

Or served us, in the restaurant.

The notion of paying attention is a recurring motif in this book and mealtimes are the perfect lay-by in the daily race to pause, reflect and give thanks.

To say grace, as they used to say. Or simply to pause and hold a moment of silent gratitude.

74

Disorientate yourself

By the rivers of Babylon,
There we sat down, yea, we wept,
When we remembered Zion.

We hanged our harps upon the willows in the
midst thereof
For there they that carried us away captive
required of us a song;
and they that wasted us required of us mirth,
saying, Sing us one of the songs of Zion.
How shall we sing the Lord's song in a
strange land?[1]

If you're thinking these are the words of a
1970s disco hit from Boney M, you're wrong.
And you're also right. The words are those of
Psalm 137, one of a collection of 150 ancient
poems sometimes called *the Psalter* and
among the most beautiful and resonant of
the Hebrew and Christian scriptures. But it
was Boney M, in the 1970s, who popularised
a reggae song by The Melodians, 'Rivers of
Babylon', that drew on the psalm.

It's a lament of those Jews exiled from the
land of their birth after the Babylonians
took Jerusalem, some six centuries before
the birth of Jesus. The Psalms are among
those ancient sacred writings which seem
to continually refresh themselves for new
generations. For example, the rebirth of
the psalm as a reggae number had special
resonance for Rastafarians, for whom the
word 'Babylon' had come to suggest any
oppressive regime. But the song also drew
from a famous line in another psalm, the
nineteenth: 'Let the words of my mouth, and
the meditation of my heart, be acceptable in
thy sight.'

The venerable collection of poetry
captures some of the most common human
experiences from fears to ecstasies, from
despair to our joy. Originally, psalms were
sung as the people gathered to worship

and many envisage a time when the
divine presence is universally understood,
when the sacred in every story is finally
recognised. But nor do they flinch from the
basest human instincts, as the singer Nick
Cave observed, reflecting on how they had
inspired his songwriting: 'I found the Psalms,
which deal directly with the relationship
between man and God, teeming with all the
clamorous desperation, longing, exaltation,
erotic violence and brutality that I could
hope for.'[2]

If the Psalms have inspired gospel songs and
hymns perhaps, argues U2's Bono, they're
even more influential in the story of the
blues: 'That's what a lot of the psalms feel
like to me, the blues. Man shouting at God:
"My God, my God, why hast thou forsaken
me? Why art thou so far from helping me?"
(Psalm 22). *The Psalter* may be a font of
gospel music, but for me it's despair that the
psalmist really reveals and the nature of his
special relationship with God. Honesty, even
to the point of anger. "How long, Lord? Wilt
thou hide thyself forever?" (Psalm 89), or
"Answer me when I call" (Psalm 5).'[3]

Leonard Cohen, Nick Cave, Bono, Mavis
Staples, Bob Dylan, Jessi Colter... Countless
artists find inspiration in the Psalms and
have taken to writing their own.

The biblical scholar Walter Brueggemann
says a psalm may do one of three things to
a reader. Sometimes a psalm will orientate
you – remind you where you're going.
Sometimes it will disorientate you – turn
you upside down. Sometimes it will utterly
re-orientate you. That's when it gives us
another way of seeing, suggests another road
to take: 'Though I walk through the valley of
the shadow of death, I will fear no evil: for
thou art with me; thy rod and thy staff they
comfort me.'[4]

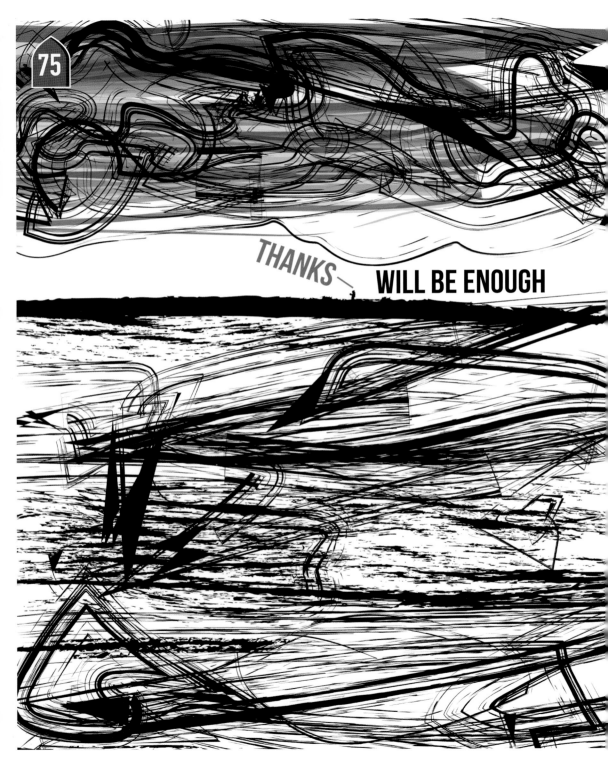

THANKS WILL BE ENOUGH

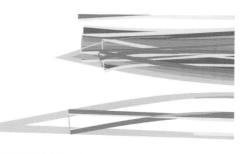

We're taught as children to say please and thank you. But, when you recognise life as a gift, this becomes about more than good manners.

It's about:
How the sun rises again.
Or how that mother cares for her child.
How two strangers meet and find they were made for each other.
A walk by the sea in winter.
Those countries at war, how they made peace.
The roar of the crowd at a match.
A bass riff...
... a bag of chips.

If we consciously notice that life is a gift, it cultivates gratitude, which helps us sense the generosity that surrounds us: in the people who came before us who made the world we take for granted. In the invisible people across this world who produce the food and clothes and gadgets we rely on. In the visible people we work with and live with who illuminate our lives with kindness or patience or loyalty or trust.

In our best selves even, how we made it to here... how we're not so bad after all.

Verbalising gratitude helps embed it in our ways of living. In their later years, the politician Denis Healey and his wife Edna, would stroll round their garden and say to one another: 'AWL' That was their shorthand for, 'Aren't We Lucky?'[1] It was how they reminded each other that they were grateful.

Thanks can even contain a hint of defiance – being grateful for the light in life even when the dark attempts to extinguish it... 'thank you we are saying and waving dark though it is...'[2] is how the poet W. S. Merwin puts it.

A dumbstruck glance at the night-time stars. A grace before a meal. A folding of the hands. An inward smile. The trickle of a tear at the funeral of a friend. A muttered prayer that we don't even understand ourselves.

As the mediaeval philosopher Meister Eckhart put it: 'If the only prayer you ever pray is "thanks", that will be enough.'

THANKS

Listen
with the night falling we are saying thank you
we are stopping on the bridges to bow from the railings
we are running out of the glass rooms
with our mouths full of food to look at the sky
and say thank you
we are standing by the water thanking it
standing by the windows looking out
in our directions

back from a series of hospitals back from a mugging
after funerals we are saying thank you
after the news of the dead
whether or not we knew them we are saying thank you

over telephones we are saying thank you
in doorways and in the backs of cars and in elevators
remembering wars and the police at the door
and the beatings on stairs we are saying thank you
in the banks we are saying thank you
in the faces of the officials and the rich
and of all who will never change
we go on saying thank you thank you

with the animals dying around us
our lost feelings we are saying thank you
with the forests falling faster than the minutes
of our lives we are saying thank you
with the words going out like cells of a brain
with the cities growing over us
we are saying thank you faster and faster
with nobody listening we are saying thank you
thank you we are saying and waving
dark though it is[3]

W. S. MERWIN

76

Get
religion

'That's me in the corner... losing my religion.'[1] An unlikely theme for an unlikely song, REM's 'Losing My Religion' is actually a play on a popular expression in the southern US for losing your cool.

But it could easily have been an anthem for an entire movement. People who actually were losing their faith – or at least coming clean that they didn't have one, and they were good with that. 'We're not here to tell you how to live your life,' reads the introduction to the charter of Sunday Assembly. 'We're here to help you be the best version of you you can be.' A secular congregation that 'celebrates life', Sunday Assembly is a religious group which... isn't religious. It was founded by a couple of comedians, Sanderson Jones and Pippa Evans, who wanted to do something that was like church but entirely secular and inclusive. It has no doctrine ('We have no set texts so we can make use of wisdom from all sources'), and no deity ('We don't do supernatural but we also won't tell you you're wrong if you do').[2]

According to research from Professor Linda Woodhead of Lancaster University, more people in Britain now say they have no religion (46 per cent) than identify with Christianity (44 per cent). She calls them the 'nones', and says 'no religion is the new norm'. The 'nones', she says, aren't hostile to faith or against religion, it just doesn't do it for them.[3]

Many people who've come to believe that life can make perfectly good sense without a deity, have also decided they don't need to waste energy in attacking those who do do God. Philosopher Alain de Botton says that, far from attacking religion, agnostics and atheists should be plundering it.

Instead of lamenting how it's scientifically implausible they should celebrate how it's psychologically helpful. Faith traditions, he says, are ripe with resources for living and organising society, bursting with insight into how to build community, strengthen relationships, appreciate art and overcome our feelings of inadequacy. Even if you've lost your religion.

What religion has discovered must be decoupled from its supernatural moorings so that everyone else can use it to stay afloat on life's choppy waters. 'The wisdom of the faiths,' he writes in *Religion for Atheists*, 'belongs to all of mankind, even the most rational among us, and deserves to be selectively reabsorbed by the supernatural's greatest enemies'.[4]

77

Make yourself up

You get up in the morning and do what you normally do.

It's what you always do. It's become your life.

But something inside you tells you this is not the thing you want to be doing. It just isn't *you*.

It's not even that it's the wrong thing, just that it's not the right thing. It's not all of who you are. Or even most.

'What should I do with my life?' That's the question you'd ask yourself if that sense of vague unease were ever articulate enough to become a question.

Half of British people, according to one survey, would take a pay cut in exchange for a job which gave them a sense of self-worth. Two thirds were 'unfulfilled or drifting'. A vague sense of disappointment with our paid work can hit all of us at different times – and even thinking about options can be seen as a luxury when millions of other people toil long hours in field or factory just to put food on the table or a child through school.

But asking what we should do with our lives isn't a question that is just confined to our job. It is also about how we are built as people and how we become ourselves.

At one time this kind of thing was called a vocation – from the Latin *vocare*, meaning 'call'. And if you believed in God, as most people in that time did, the question was about what God was calling you to do. People had visions. They heard voices. The literature of faith is rammed with God-Direct – instant divine messaging which leaves people with little uncertainty about what to do next.

For most of us things are fuzzier. 'You have been given questions to which you cannot be given answers,' says the poet Wendell Berry. 'You will have to live them out – perhaps a little at a time.'[1]

We might need to reframe the questions. Asking what we're good at, what brings us fulfilment, where we find ourselves. This is how we can make ourselves up.

But none of us find this out quickly. Or finally. The writer Po Bronson interviewed 900 people who had switched from one path in life to another: a stockbroker who became a fish farmer; an estate agent who opened a craft factory in Central America; a lawyer who became a priest. The call, he found, crept up on people, over time, bit by bit, usually hedged around with doubt and fear. There was never any writing on the wall, only a feeling in the gut. 'Most of us don't get epiphanies,' says Bronson. 'We only get a whisper – a faint urge. That's it. That's the call. It's up to you to do the work of discovery, to connect it to an answer.'[2]

The false starts and detours are all part of how we get there, how we become ourselves. No one expresses this better than Caitlin Moran in her novel *How to Build a Girl*:

There is no academy where you can learn to be yourself; there is no line manager, slowly urging you towards the right answer. You are midwife to yourself and will give birth to yourself over and over in dark rooms alone.

And some versions of you will end in dismal failure – many prototypes won't even get out of the front door.

Until – slowly, slowly – you make a viable version of you, one you can hum every day. You'll find the tiny right piece of grit you can pearl around until nature kicks in and your shell will just quietly fill with magic even while you're busy doing other things. What your nurture began, nature will take over and start completing.[3]

78

Shhhh...

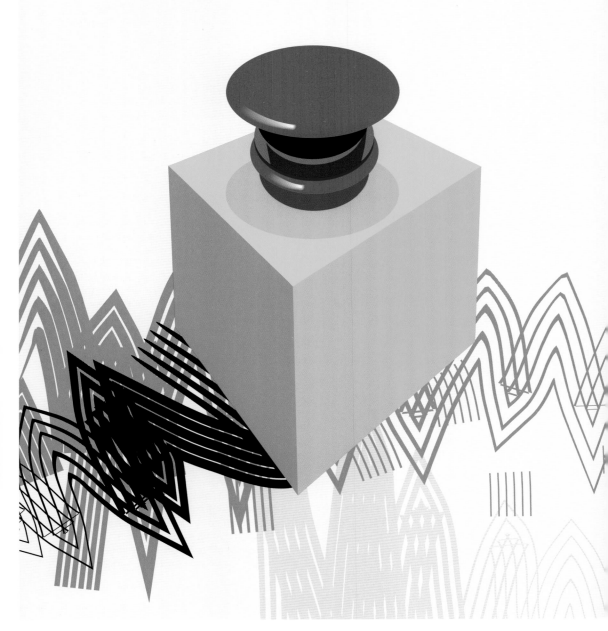

It was the seventeenth-century French philosopher Blaise Pascal who wrote that 'All men's miseries derive from not being able to sit quietly in a room alone.'

Although Blaise sounds a bit of a misery guts, perhaps he was onto something. In an experiment reported in the journal *Science*, researchers at the University of Virginia invited forty people to sit alone in an empty room for twenty minutes. No electronic gadgets allowed, not even a watch. They were shown a button, which, if pressed, would give them an electrical shock. Everyone gave it a practice press and received a practice shock – ouch. Everyone vowed they'd pay money to avoid receiving that shock again.

Then they were asked to sit still with their own thoughts and not fall asleep. At the end of the study most people reported how difficult it was, even unpleasant. Just sitting there, doing nothing. Two-thirds of the men and a quarter of the women found their own company so troubling that they chose the electric shock treatment.[1]

We all want stimulation. We long to be needed. We're said to live in an 'age of distraction', perhaps it's because we like it that way. We're unsure of what we might find if we stopped to look. If we turned inward, instead of always turning outward. Perhaps we confuse being alone with being lonely.

We might be mistaken. An intentional solitude can be like a wakeful sleep. Just as sleep helps the mind to process and organise the chaos of thought – so that sometimes we wake up with a clarity we couldn't find before – so sitting alone in quiet, determining to resist the distractions, can be regenerative. It can renew our friendship with our own selves. It can orientate us by locating us. It can calm us.

When we choose a period of solitude, there is nothing to fear. At the kitchen table, with the radio turned off. In the bedroom, when everyone else has left the flat, smartphone out of reach. Or even a short lunchtime walk from the office in a busy town, turning through the doors of that building you rarely look twice at.

'Two years ago I was being cross-questioned in a court case in London,' said Michael Palin, writer and former Monty Python member: 'During a lunch break in which I was not permitted to talk to anyone, I desperately wanted somewhere to sit quietly and get myself together. And yet there was nowhere where the price of a seat didn't involve eating, drinking or some commercial transaction. Then, out of the blue, at the very heart of Fleet Street, I discovered the church of St Dunstan-in-the-West. I was never so grateful for a place of repose, an oasis of peace and quiet in the midst of the mayhem.'[2]

In the furious activity of a world where the volume is turned up, houses of worship may be just the place to sit quietly and alone, to hear the silence speak.

'Churches are vessels of hush, as well as everything else they are,' says the writer Francis Spufford. 'And when I block out the distractions of vision, the silence is almost shockingly loud.'[3]

79

Share this
bread

Bread is wonderful. Think of the extraordinary number of different shapes and forms it comes in. Crusty French sticks, all airy in the middle; warm doughy naan; Arabic flatbread, pizza; damp white slices built for a bacon sarnie. Challah, anyone?

Bread is a staple for many people across the globe. No wonder that it's become a powerful symbol and metaphor. It stands for something elemental. Bread comes out of an organic process of life and death, the seed goes into the ground and dies. It is reborn as wheat, then cut down, and the grain ground into flour. Then yeast brings it alive once more, as the goodness of the grain is released in the making and baking. We eat, and excrete and it returns to the earth. It's a life cycle.

'All bread,'[1] writes Margaret Atwood:

... is made of wood,
cow dung, packed brown moss,
the bodies of dead animals, the teeth
and backbones, what is left
after the ravens. This dirt
flows through the stems into the grain,
into the arm,...

'Bread is the staff of life', as the saying goes.

Jesus called himself 'the bread of life' and in the Christian rite of Eucharist people share bread and say: 'Though we are many, we are one body, because we all share in one bread.'

Wherever we are on the belief spectrum, this idea of being unified through food is built into our lives.

The word 'company' – from the Latin *cum* ('with') and *panis* ('bread') – means sharing bread. A companion is someone you share bread with. A company is (or maybe should be) a group that eats together. We all share in one bread. Margaret Atwood says it like this:

to know what you devour
is to consecrate it,
almost. All bread must be broken
so it can be shared. Together,
we eat this earth.[2]

Food is a kind of binding agent – social glue. The sharing of food is at the heart of hospitality. The welcoming of the stranger is core to the practice of cultures and religions the world over. Shared food, and the conversation that comes with it, become the means of breaking down ethnic and cultural barriers. Turning strangers into friends.

80

Become your best self

A woman lies under a summer sun, soaking up the rays. Slowly, she becomes aware that she is not alone. She notices the faintest of movement on her hand. A tiny grasshopper has landed. As she observes the precision of its movement, notes its fragile beauty, she becomes aware of the wonder of every fleeting day, the passing nature of time itself.

It was one such ordinary moment that was transfigured into an unlikely epiphany for the Pulitzer-winning poet Mary Oliver, sparking the deepest of questions in her poem 'The Summer Day': What are we going to do with this precious life we find ourselves living?

That's what poets do, look twice at the apparently ordinary in the belief it might take us somewhere extra-ordinary. It's a fine thing to lie under the sun and watch the world go by. But then the sun goes down, and when it next rises we have to get back to work – to put food on the table and pay for the roof over our heads.

But work is more than paying the bills. It's how we make our mark in life. How we show to our peers that we were here, and we made the most of it. When we're up for a job, the evidence on our CV is what the American columnist David Brooks, in *The Road to Character*, calls our 'résumé virtues' – accomplishments in education and career that witness our external achievements in this life; that signal our status. Everything from our exam results to our progress at the company, the skills we develop and the salary we take home.

Our culture lays high store by our CV, but, as the saying goes, 'Nobody will say on their deathbed, "I wish I'd spent more time at the office".' Brooks noticed another set of virtues, the kind of values he found in the lives of people who radiated an 'inner light'. This parallel set of qualifications he called

'eulogy virtues' – what people might say about you when you die.

At your funeral, no one will mention your exam results. The hours you spent at work. Your title or salary. They will remember another edition of your life. He was a father who loved playing with his kids. She was a neighbour who'd always ask after your health. She was generous and patient. He was loyal and brave. You could trust her.

Eulogy virtues are hard to measure, but easier to witness. They're not about your qualifications in life but the quality of your life. They are a glue that holds families and friendships together, that help us negotiate life's toughest tests.

The best eulogy recalls someone who recognised their human flaws, and tried to face them down. Are we mean or consumed with envy? Do we hold grudges? Can we compromise? Can we forgive? Do we ever shut up and let others speak?

Often, says Brooks, we are more focused on building an external career than on building inner character:

But if we live for external achievement, years pass and our deepest parts go unexplored and unstructured. You lack a moral vocabulary. It is easy to slip into a self-satisfied moral mediocrity. You grade yourself on a forgiving curve. You figure as long as you are not obviously hurting anybody and people seem to like you, you must be OK. But you live with an unconscious boredom, separated from the deepest meaning of life and the highest moral joys. Gradually, a humiliating gap opens between your actual self and your desired self, between you and those incandescent souls you sometimes meet.[1]

We're not here for long. Witness the grasshopper, next time one lands on your hand.

81

Take the overview

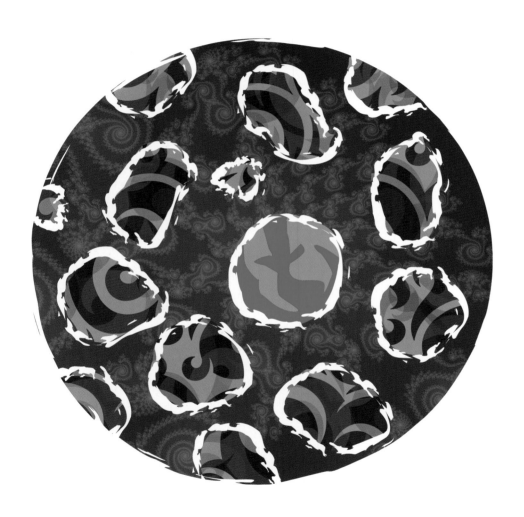

There are 7.5 billion of us sharing this planet. We live on seven continents, connected by five oceans. We speak 6,000 different languages, with Mandarin Chinese the most popular (1.2 billion speakers) or English, if you include those who speak a second language.

We disagree over everything: from the way we organise society, to which football team we support; from our religious traditions, to the food we eat. We can be suspicious and fearful – of people of another colour, of another sexual orientation, of another culture.

Ever since Cain and Abel (sons of the mythical first family of Adam and Eve) had a domestic dispute, and Cain murdered Abel, we've turned to violence to win our arguments. We're not good at peaceful resolution of our disputes. According to *The New York Times*, humans have been entirely at peace for only 268 years in the past 3,400 – that's 8 per cent of recorded history: 'Estimates for the total number killed in wars throughout all of human history range from 150 million to 1 billion.'[1]

We need to get some perspective. A different view of the planet we share. And for the first time in history, that's possible. In 1987 the writer Frank White, after speaking with twenty-nine astronauts, came up with the 'overview effect' theory. Seeing Earth from space, he argued, transforms both understanding of yourself and of your world. The astronaut begins to think of Earth as a 'shared home' and develops a sense of awe.[2]

For example, Edgar Mitchell, an astronaut on Apollo 14, described his emotions as 'interconnected euphoria'. He said: 'Something happens to you out there. You develop an instant global consciousness, a people orientation, an intense dissatisfaction with the state of the world, and a compulsion to do something about it. From out there on the moon, international politics look so petty. You want to grab a politician by the scruff of the neck and drag him a quarter of a million miles out and say, "Look at that, you son of a bitch."'[3]

In *Overview* (a film made by Planetary Collective), Nicole Stott, an astronaut on the International Space Station, put it like this: 'We have this connection to Earth. I mean, it's our home. And I don't know how you can come back and not, in some way, be changed.'[4]

Ron Garan, who also spent time on the space station, described his new way of seeing: 'When we look down at the earth from space, we see this amazing, indescribably beautiful planet. It looks like a living, breathing organism. But it also, at the same time, looks extremely fragile.'[5]

As William Anders, one of the first three people to have left earth's orbit and travelled to the moon, said: 'We came all this way to explore the moon, and the most important thing is that we discovered the earth.'[6]

82

Light a
candle

A famous entertainer endures the final days of illness: she's 'in our thoughts and prayers'. A family we know face tragedy: 'Our thoughts and prayers are with them.' Innocent civilians, caught in a war zone: 'They're in our thoughts and prayers.'

It's the catch-all, go-to phrase for public figures who rarely use the vocabulary of faith. A politician, for example, puts 'thoughts' in front of 'prayers' to moderate the religious aspect. They want to convey empathy without pretending that they – or we – are as devout as we once were.

Sometimes the 'prayer' word is dropped completely. Sending 'all strength, thoughts and best wishes'. It's the thought that counts, even when our words can feel like they don't count for much. If we can't honestly pray for someone, we can let them know we're thinking well of them.

The roots of the phrase 'thoughts and prayers' go back to 1821, and the *Christian Herald and Seaman's Magazine*, sadly no longer on sale. 'Masters and seamen,' writes the author, 'as you are about to leave us for the season, I trust we shall follow you in our thoughts and prayers.'[1] Doubtless they did, and the expression had more than sea legs.

Finding the right words is tricky in an age of religious diversity – acknowledging the possibility of faith without alienating those who don't share it.

All of us do thoughts, but we don't all do prayer. At least not in the way people have often thought of prayer, as communication with an unseen power in a manner which transforms our experience of life. But there is a kind of prayer that doesn't ask whether or not God exists, but understands that contemplation and reflection are in themselves transformative.

The twentieth-century French painter Henri Matisse wasn't sure if he believed in God, but late in life he designed a small chapel for the Dominican sisters in the town of Vence on the French Riviera. He said: 'I don't know whether I believe in God or not. I think, really, I'm some sort of Buddhist. But the essential thing is to put oneself in a frame of mind which is close to that of prayer.'[2]

Sometimes we overrate belief and underplay experience, but the practice of prayer can transcend any creed. On those days when we can't find the words for what is happening in our lives or in our world maybe all we can do is:

Light a solitary candle on the kitchen table.

Stand without words in a two-minute silence.

Lay a flower at the roadside.

Bow in respect as the funeral cortege goes by.

Sometimes a prayer is as simple as this poem, by Michael Leunig:

These circumstances will change. This situation shall pass. *Amen.*[3]

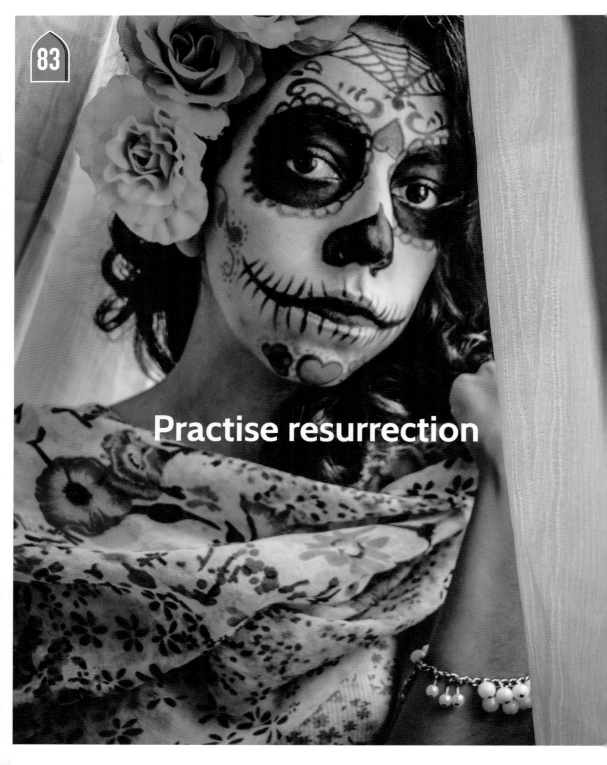

83

Practise resurrection

It would be good if death was not the end of us. If, when we breathe our last, this veil of tears is drawn back to reveal some beautiful welcome of peace, love and understanding. Death will always ask us to wonder whether our end is *the* end. As Shakespeare's Hamlet says:

For in that sleep of death what dreams may come
When we have shuffled off this mortal coil,
Must give us pause.

But none of us know what comes next. Or even if, after we've identified our coil and shuffled off it, a next event comes. Still, we have those dreams. And longings, for something more. Perhaps it's simply the rude implausibility of accepting that someone we know so dearly – their looks and ways of speaking, the times we shared, their loves and hates – can simply cease to be. It's as difficult to believe they're gone as to believe they aren't.

Maybe our instinct is evolutionary, the witness of nature; how every year the life of the earth falls with the seasons into sleep, before rising into life, hungry for the light. Humans have always cherished notions of a life beyond death. Or of resurrection, returning from death to this life. From stories of a deity who dies and rises, to the belief that everyone will be present as history's final credits roll. A reckoning. A Last Judgement. Blinking and rubbing his eyes, say the Christians, Jesus of Nazareth walked out of the tomb on the third day, a promise that 'death has lost its sting'.

But, truth be told, death still stings.

Like nothing else.

And, with or without faith, there's no way to be sure, if he did, or didn't. Our certainties are restricted to life before death, which has its own discrete resurrection qualities.

Put your faith in the two inches of humus
that will build under the trees
every thousand years

says Wendell Berry, inviting his readers to 'Practice resurrection': 'Be joyful though you have considered all the facts.'[1]

And how do you find joy after considering all the facts? The Franciscan Richard Rohr says one way to practise resurrection is to practise life now as we would want to practise life in the kind of world we can only dream about. Here's ten of his suggestions:

1 *Refuse to identify with negative, blaming, antagonistic, or fearful thoughts (you cannot stop 'having' them).*

2 *Apologise when you hurt another person or situation.*

3 *Undo your mistakes by some positive action toward the offended person or situation.*

4 *Always seek to change yourself before trying to change others.*

5 *Choose as much as possible to serve rather than be served.*

6 *Whenever possible, seek the common good over your mere private good.*

7 *Give preference to those in pain, excluded, or disabled in any way.*

8 *Seek just systems and policies over mere charity.*

9 *Make sure your medium is the same as your message.*

10 *Never doubt that it is all about love in the end.*[2]

84

Put down
roots

Love is a temporary madness, it erupts like volcanoes and then subsides. And when it subsides you have to make a decision. You have to work out whether your roots have so entwined together that it is inconceivable that you should ever part. Because this is what love is. Love is not breathlessness, it is not excitement, it is not the promulgation of eternal passion. That is just being 'in love', which any fool can do. Love itself is what is left over when being in love has burned away, and this is both an art and a fortunate accident. Those that truly love, have roots that grow towards each other underground, and when all the pretty blossom have fallen from their branches, they find that they are one tree and not two.[1]

LOUIS DE BERNIÈRES

85

Live your way into a new kind of thinking

In the twenty-first century, the great faith traditions are caught up in a long-running argument over what their adherents believe. We hear about people of faith, not because of what they do, but because of what they believe. Or don't.

Are they comfortable with gays and lesbians? Do women have the same rights as men? Is there a dress code? Do miracles happen? Do the findings of science contradict religion? Or complement it? Is a holy book prescriptive? Or for general guidance?

Take Christianity. The Church has taught that if we can get our beliefs right then we'll be able to get our actions right. Orthodoxy leads to orthopraxis. Otherwise there will be weeping and gnashing of teeth, which will require orthodontistry. The Church is big on crossing the Ts and dotting the Is.

While religion often oversells doctrine it often undersells community and friendship. Theologian Ann Morisy noticed that Jesus

didn't say 'I speak the way', or, 'I believe the way'. He said: 'I am the way.' He didn't say 'I'll speak true words to you', or, 'I'll tell you about the truth', but, 'I am the truth'.[1]

He saw truth in relationships and friendship, not in facts and dogma. If you wanted to know truth you needed to become friends and the community of those friends eventually got called 'Church'.

Tempting though it is for educated people to argue about religion a lot, the benefits of faith are found not in the speculating but in the participating. Not in the theory but in the practical.

It's better to *do* religion than to *think* religion. And practising is the only way to believe it. If you can't believe your way into faith, you can practise your way. This was captured by the Dutch Catholic writer Henri Nouwen who said: 'You don't think your way into a new kind of living. You live your way into a new kind of thinking.'[2]

86

Let evening come

Photographers and filmmakers call it 'the Golden Hour'. That moment, just before the sun rises or sets, when the light is softer and warmer than at any other time in the day.

Emmanuel 'Chivo' Lubezki, the Oscar-winning cinematographer on *The Revenant*, insisted on shooting the film only in this short window of dwindling daylight. 'We shot for an hour and a half only at the end of the day,' explained the movie's star Leonardo DiCaprio. 'As they say, you know, "that's when God speaks".'[1]

The quality of light distinguishes these twilight moments early in the morning and late in the evening. They also form a kind of buffer zone between night and day, between day and night. This borderland is more than meteorological or chronological; it has emotional, spiritual and artistic echoes too.

Anticipating daybreak or nightfall, we might feel trepidation or excitement. The daily cycle calls to mind a world of beginnings and endings: of natural ebb and flow, but also transitions in relationships, career, location; entrances and exits, birth and death.

In the morning twilight, on a good day, you may take a deep breath, and allow the imagination to send out its search parties – sending signals, making connections. That first cup of tea steaming in your hand, the day's prospects unfurl before you. As Denise Levertov puts it in 'Variation on a Theme by Rilke', the day ahead becomes a challenge, a dare:

A certain day became a presence to me...

... it leaned over
and struck my shoulder as if with
the flat of a sword, granting me
honor and a task. The day's blow
rang out, metallic – or it was I, a bell awakened,
and what I heard was my whole self
saying and singing what it knew: I can.[2]

As the misty half-light grows more luminous, as those scurrying scouting parties of the wakening imagination report back, more often than not, you begin to see possibilities. Just supposing... what if... here's a thought...

The golden hour, when the light speaks to you.

87

EVERYBODY WORSHIPS

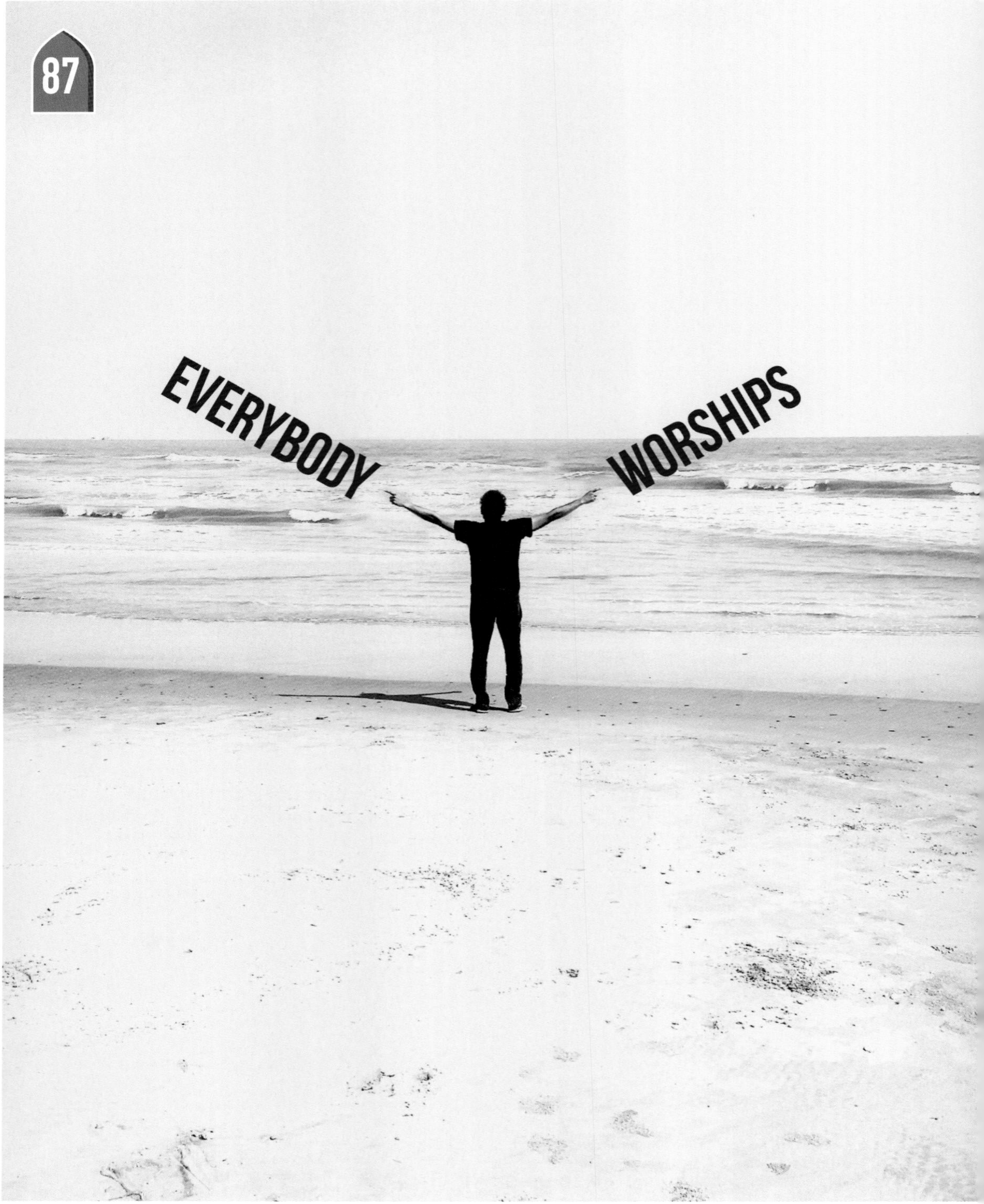

In the day-to-day trenches of adult life, there is actually no such thing as atheism. There is no such thing as not worshipping. Everybody worships. The only choice we get is what to worship. And an outstanding reason for choosing some sort of God or spiritual-type thing to worship – be it JC or Allah, be it Yahweh or the Wiccan mother-goddess or the Four Noble Truths or some infrangible set of ethical principles – is that pretty much anything else you worship will eat you alive. If you worship money and things – if they are where you tap real meaning in life – then you will never have enough. Never feel you have enough. It's the truth. Worship your own body and beauty and sexual allure and you will always feel ugly, and when time and age start showing, you will die a million deaths before they finally plant you. On one level, we all know this stuff already – it's been codified as myths, proverbs, clichés, bromides, epigrams, parables: the skeleton of every great story. The trick is keeping the truth up-front in daily consciousness. Worship power – you will feel weak and afraid, and you will need ever more power over others to keep the fear at bay. Worship your intellect, being seen as smart – you will end up feeling stupid, a fraud, always on the verge of being found out. And so on.

Look, the insidious thing about these forms of worship is not that they're evil or sinful; it is that they are unconscious.

They are default settings. They're the kind of worship you just gradually slip into, day after day, getting more and more selective about what you see and how you measure value without ever being fully aware that that's what you're doing. And the world will not discourage you from operating on your default settings, because the world of men and money and power hums along quite nicely on the fuel of fear and contempt and frustration and craving and the worship of self. Our own present culture has harnessed these forces in ways that have yielded extraordinary wealth and comfort and personal freedom. The freedom to be lords of our own tiny skull-sized kingdoms, alone at the center of all creation. This kind of freedom has much to recommend it. But of course there are all different kinds of freedom, and the kind that is most precious you will not hear much talked about in the great outside world of winning and achieving and displaying. The really important kind of freedom involves attention, and awareness, and discipline, and effort, and being able truly to care about other people and to sacrifice for them, over and over, in myriad petty little unsexy ways, every day. That is real freedom. The alternative is unconsciousness, the default-setting, the 'rat race' – the constant gnawing sense of having had and lost some infinite thing...

DAVID FOSTER WALLACE[1]

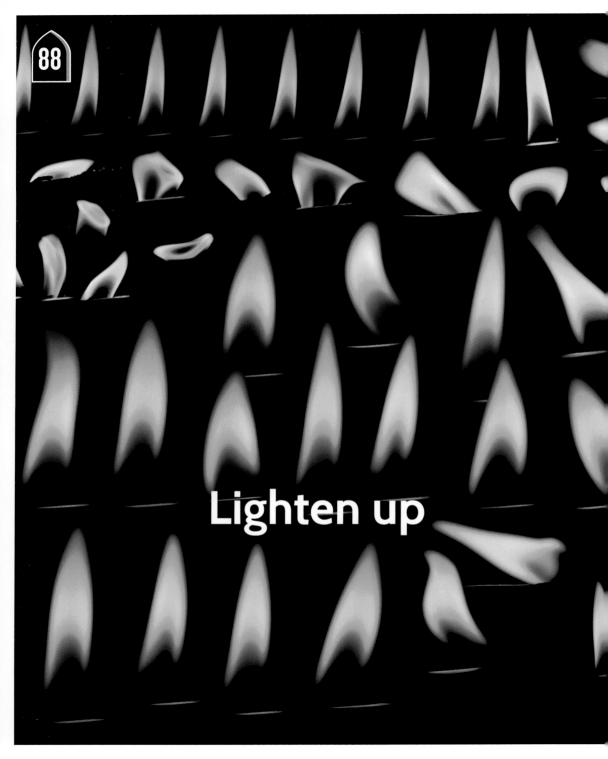

88

Lighten up

'It's better to light a candle than to curse the darkness.' Well, up to a point. Cursing the darkness can be quite therapeutic. Unleashing a primal scream. Letting it all out. Howling at the moon.

But the benefits may be short term. Ultimately, the darkness is pretty resistant to insults and cursing. The darkness is often faceless, nameless, random and not open to negotiation.

But still, darkness falls.

Our lives can put us in the way of devastating sadness. From the sudden death of a friend to an inexplicable act of terror on our streets. From a downswing in our mental wellbeing to the traumatic end of a cherished relationship. Days, weeks and months can become too difficult to process. If we ever did have words to express the deep ache of sadness we feel – for ourselves or for someone else – they long ago started sounding empty and we're tired of speaking them.

Yet even when life is pitch dark, we want to believe that it is not the end of the story.

If we don't have the words to describe how we feel, or to chart a way out, we have metaphors and among the most elemental is that of light and dark.

This is why, after some shocking act of terror, people gather in town squares after dark and light candles. And why solidarity for a group of people under threat or facing disaster is signalled by a candlelight vigil.

Why people queue solemnly at places of worship to add one more flickering flame to a shimmering crowd of illuminated candles. And why it's not a futile gesture to light a candle in our own homes, when friends gather – to declare companionship with each other, and to help find a way through the darkness.

A small, frail, wordless act of resistance in favour of life. As Archbishop Desmond Tutu – who spent his life campaigning against the darkness of apartheid – said:

Goodness is stronger than evil
love is stronger than hate
light is stronger than darkness
life is stronger than death.[1]

89

You'll never
walk alone

The Lord is my shepherd; I shall not want.
He maketh me to lie down in green pastures: he
leadeth me beside the still waters.
He restoreth my soul: he leadeth me in the paths
of righteousness for his name's sake.
Yea, though I walk through the valley of the
shadow of death, I will fear no evil: for thou
art with me; thy rod and thy staff they comfort
me.
Thou preparest a table before me in the
presence of mine enemies: thou anointest my
head with oil; my cup runneth over.
Surely goodness and mercy shall follow me
all the days of my life: and I will dwell in the
house of the Lord for ever.

For centuries, Psalm 23 has been the go-to poem for people feeling fragile or raw. It's the biblical equivalent of comfort food, or a warm blanket. And, for many of us, it works. That's why it's read so often at funerals.

Yes, it says that we're like sheep, which is a bit harsh, but part of its value is that it recognises that life isn't always straightforward. There are green pastures and still waters, but beyond them lurk the presence of enemies and the valley of the shadow of death. We get that.

What's reassuring is the notion that whatever life throws at us – good or bad – we're never left entirely alone. The psalmist found his or her comfort in the watchful presence of God. This may not be an option for everyone but we can all take real solace in close companionship.

When the birds sing and the river chuckles, we turn to our soul mates to share our pleasure. When night falls and the wolves howl, we draw each other close for comfort. In company, we can still raise a glass, even if hostile faces may press themselves against the window. Goodness and mercy are still around the table.

The Canadian singer-songwriter Jane Siberry wrote her own version of Psalm 23, called 'The Valley':

You rise every morning
Wondering what in the world will the world bring today
Will it bring you joy or will it take it away
And every step you take is guided by
The love of the light on the land and the blackbird's cry...[1]

She adds: 'You will walk in good company.' It's the best way of walking.

Michael Donaghy ends his poem 'The Present' with the words:

Make me this present then: your hand in mine, and we'll live out our lives in it.[2]

Amen, the psalmist might say.

90

Take the journey with
the dead guy

Most days, death is so far away that you can't see it. And then a day arrives when it is so close you can almost touch it.

The experience of loss that it brings is so unlike any other human experience that it can feel like the end of everything. But, in some surreal twist, everything carries on anyway.

'The days of our life are threescore years and ten,' reads the good book. 'And if by reason of strength they be fourscore years yet... it is soon cut off, and we fly away.'[1] We might be lucky; we might get a good long life but it too will be cut off. Death is a frame hung around our days to give us a sense of perspective which, most of the time, we'd rather not have.

In the past, the healthiest versions of religion offered a way of navigating the arrival of death with beliefs and rites that were unembarrassed by our mortality, and offered a hope that this is not the end. Someone's death might be marked in an elaborate public ritual, the whole community participating. But that's less easy when many of us no longer buy into religion in the same way, or feel the need to rely on the advice of a religious professional, particularly one selling their own brand. At the same time, Western society has privatised death. Previously, the dead person lay in the home and people could come and pay their respects, but we have become embarrassed about the dead body, hiding it away in hospital morgue or funeral parlour.

With the waning of a religious framework to mark someone's passing, funeral services can morph into extended tributes, celebrations of a person's passions marked by witty stories and familiar music. But the shock of death demands some gravity in order to hold our grief; some silence to contain an unspeakable loss.

Our fear of the dead body and the absence of a traditional narrative risks depriving us of the serious journey of grief. That's the argument of the undertaker and poet Thomas Lynch, the inspiration behind the hit American TV show *Six Feet Under*, about a funeral home. Lynch says that we shouldn't fear taking the journey with the dead guy; that, where possible, loved ones should get involved with the physical disposal of the body in cremation or burial. A 'good funeral' is not just about remembering the person we've lost but recognising the permanence of this loss in each of us who remain. By getting the dead where they need to go, the living get where they need to be.

'Whatever's there to feel, feel it,' writes Lynch, '– the riddance, the relief, the fright and freedom, the fear of forgetting, the dull ache of your own mortality. Get with someone you can trust with tears, with anger, and wonderment and utter silence. Get that part done – the sooner the better. The only way around these things is through them.'[2]

91

Replay the day

The Greek philosopher Plato, living around 400 years before Jesus, recorded the words of another philosopher, Socrates, when he said: 'The unexamined life is not worth living.'

Is it snobbish and elitist to suggest that people who aren't reading the latest scrolls, or boring each other to tears about obscure philosophical issues, are wasting their days? We could give Socrates the benefit of doubt and say he was exaggerating to make a point, but still, a lot of people seem perfectly happy not looking at life too closely as it passes.

Some of us fear what we might find (maybe, once, we did stop to look). Or we convince ourselves we're too busy for self-reflection (it's on the list – for later). Perhaps we see ourselves as more about action than reflection, more about *doing* than *being*. That might explain why we haven't really reflected on our lack of reflection.

But whatever we think about the unexamined life, many people find that an examined one can be surprisingly rewarding: taking a moment to stop and notice what we're doing with our time. A day contains 1,440 minutes. Putting aside five for a moment of review may transform the other 1,435. A practice like this might be called meditation, or mindfulness. It might be called prayer.

The Jesuits, a Catholic order founded by Ignatius of Loyola in the sixteenth century, picked up early on the idea of a daily playback. Ignatius created a series of spiritual exercises designed to help people deepen their experience. One of these – conducting a slo-mo replay of the day's action – can enrich anyone's life. It's called 'the Examen', or sometimes a 'consciousness examination'. It's a simple, daily life check. The kind of exercise we can do each night before bed; reminding ourselves that this day, like all the rest, is a bit of a jigsaw. Considering the shape of some of the pieces might help put it all together. Examining our life might help shape it. 'How we spend our days is how we spend our lives,'[1] as Annie Dillard says.

The Examen has five steps:

Give thanks. Replay the day you've had, freeze-frame the people or moments you're grateful for.

Capture some sign of hope or joy. Was there a moment of forgiveness or compassion? A sign of courage or unexpected love? Often we notice these moments only in retrospect.

Notice any sadness or regret. Some news you heard about or event you were part of? Some word you regret or action you neglected?

Recognise the down as well as the up. Acknowledge the bad as well as the good.

Consider tomorrow. In light of all this, how might it be different?

Rewind.

Hit play.

Watch the day again.

What was good, what was not? Examine your life. There is no test. Life is all course work.

92

Make your
mark

'Why do you wear that cross round your neck?' Ask that question to a handful of people and the answer may be different every time. As it would to a group of people wearing a hijab, or a yarmulke.

These physical markers are signs of something which is largely invisible. Tattoos, tribal scars and badges can have a similar symbolic power, saying something about our spiritual, emotional or political allegiances. But not saying everything. And the meaning may shift, depending on whether someone wants to stand out... or fit in. A Muslim may describe her hijab as a signal that she is not owned by society, that her ultimate allegiance lies elsewhere. But these signatures go beyond religion. We have a kind of nesting instinct to populate our lives with signs and markers of what we value. We treasure photographs of loved ones, together with mementos of memorable experiences: a pebble carried home from a beach, a kitsch souvenir from a holiday resort. Hanging on a wall or sitting in a fireplace, they're domestic versions of prayer shrines with their icons and candles. We make our nests mobile – carrying around familiar emblems in our wallets, purses and phones.

When someone we love dies, and we're faced with the clearance of their belongings, there are heart-rending decisions to make. What to sell, what to give away, what to junk and what to keep. The mementoes we decide to hold on to may have no financial value, but they're rich in meaning and memory. A brooch, scarf, book or pipe which is redolent with personal history. These objects are significant – physical bulwarks against forgetting. They bring someone who has died back to life, and keep them alive in our hearts. They make the invisible visible.

This investment in physical symbols is deeper than we notice. The things we wear, the objects we hold dear, and the tokens we treat as sacred are part of our identity. They reassure us of who we are, and connect us to worlds beyond the immediate. They are *aides-memoire*, post-it-notes which remind us of the invisible threads of relationship and values that hold our lives together.

Rooted in tradition or in history they are not merely about the past. They help us negotiate the here-and-now. They are signs of life.

93

Live in the long now

In the year 01999 (1999 to the rest of us) an American foundation bought part of a mountain in eastern Nevada. In this remote area of white limestone cliffs, they planned to build an unusual kind of clock – that ticks just once a year. It would have a century hand not an hour hand, moving only once every hundred years.

The 10,000 Year Clock is the dream of inventor Danny Hillis, who believes in what musician Brian Eno calls 'The Long Now'.[1] At the Long Now Foundation, they see time differently. They want to signal that life is not about speed but being present, not about faster and cheaper, but slower and deeper. None of them will live to see the hands on the clock move, but that's okay because the 10,000 Year Clock takes the long view.

It's the same perspective as the fourteenth-century founders of New College Oxford. The college dining hall was made with a series of oak beams across the ceiling, which, half a millennium later, by the end of the nineteenth century, had become infested with beetles. The story goes that the college called in a man who farmed college land, who responded: 'Ah – we wondered when you might get in touch.' He told them of a tradition going back to the fourteenth century that a grove of oaks had been planted on college land to replace those cut down for the dining-hall beams. These oaks were set aside, and century after century, the farmers had waited.

Today we're less patient. We like to have things now. Our deliveries are tracked and we monitor their journeys towards us. We don't wait for changing seasons before buying particular fruit or veg, because our supermarkets ship them from different seasons across the world, ready to satisfy our demands. Waiting feels like time-wasting. Waiting times are to be reduced. Don't just stand there, we're told, do something!

But sometimes, it's only waiting that can tell us what we want or need. In the calendar of the Christian Church an entire season called Advent is given over to waiting, longing, for a new kind of world to be born. A time when time will be called on history. When time will be up.

It's a tradition that grew from the story of the Hebrew people waiting for their Messiah. A waiting which had developed since slavery in Egypt, grown through exile in Babylon, and been incubated under Roman captivity. 'A voice cries out in the wilderness,' said the prophet Isaiah, about 2,700 years ago. 'Prepare the way of the Lord, make straight in the desert a highway for our God.'[2]

It's not a passive waiting but an active one. An alert, vigilant and intentional patience which recognises that we all live in the long now, and some days history will not be fast-forwarded.

Waiting is part of being alive. Like sleep, it can't be rushed. We wait to find out who we are, and what we could do. And sometimes as we wait, we discover we are waiting for something else altogether. We understand what we are to do.

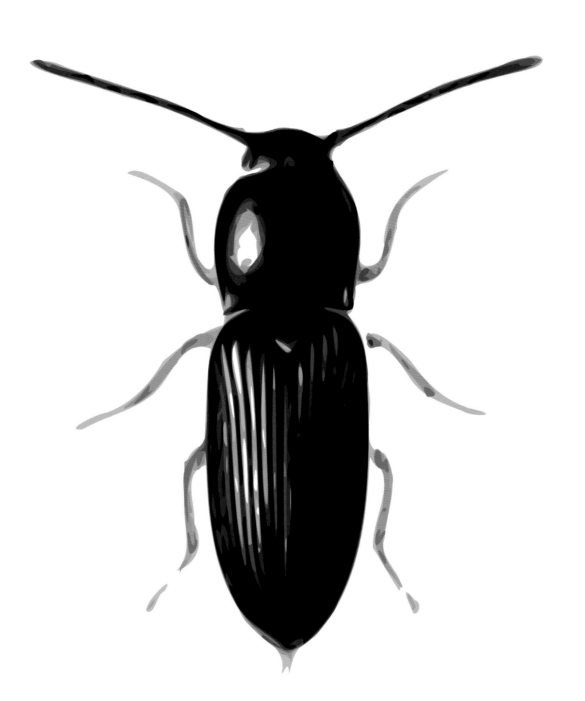

94

Believe it
or not

Back in 1563 the Church of England published its *Thirty-nine Articles of Religion*. (For example: 'we confess that vain and rash Swearing is forbidden'.) Previously, Thomas Cranmer had come up with 'The Ten Articles' ('The observance of various rites and ceremonies as good and laudable, such as clerical vestments, sprinkling of holy water, bearing of candles on Candlemas-day, giving of ashes on Ash Wednesday.'). In Germany they'd come up with six. Luckily at the time, most people couldn't read, so the priest didn't test anyone on their way into church.

Christianity has always been big on beliefs – and falling out over them. Eventually, at a Church version of the European Union, in Nicaea in AD 325, a treaty called the *Nicene Creed* was settled on. That one, or a slightly different one, the *Apostles' Creed*, is still recited in many churches. Both are full of answers to questions people were asking 1,700 years ago.

If you want to check out what kind of belie-ver you might be an online calculator 'Belief-O-Matic'[1] asks you twenty questions about your concept of God, the afterlife and human nature and then tells you your religion. But even though modern religious faith is often about what you believe, many of us find our beliefs can be a little hard to read.

'When is it that you can say you believe?' asks writer Francis Spufford: 'It's tricky, since belief is often so intermittent; is so often checkered through or stippled through with disbelief; is so much something come upon, or sensed out of the corner of the mind's eye, rather than securely possessed. Is it when you feel you've found something? Or is it much earlier: when you feel the need that will make you start looking? When you do start looking? When you fail to find

anything and yet somehow don't give up the hope that you might find something some day? Maybe it's when you hope at all, in this direction.'[2]

And anyway, the meaning of the word 'belief' has changed. Theologian Marcus Borg pointed out that in English, prior to about 1600, the verb 'believe' always had a person as its direct object, not a statement. It did not mean believing that a statement (say, 'I believe in the Virgin Birth,'), is true, but more like what we mean when we say to somebody: 'I believe in you.'

To believe *in* somebody, he said, is not the same as believing somebody. 'I believe in you' means having confidence in you – for people of faith that means having confidence in the divine. The old English *be loef* is the root of the word believe and it means 'to hold dear', and is related to the word 'belove'.

Originally the etymology of belief was about *trust*, but somewhere down the line a few centuries ago, the trust element in faith was displaced in favour of the 'mental assertion of an extremely long list of facts' element. In favour of insiders versus outsiders – those who can sign up to every line of a creed and those who can't.

Actually, said Borg, the Latin root of the word *credo* – from which we get the word creed – means 'I give my heart to'. 'Heart,' he said, 'is a metaphor for the self at its deepest level – a level of the self beneath our thinking, willing and feeling.'[3]

'Do you believe in me?' meant 'Do you belove me?'

In the end beliefs are often overrated. There is only one article of faith. Love.

95

CREATE A CLEARING

CLEARING

Do not try to save
the whole world
or do anything grandiose.
Instead, create
a clearing
in the dense forest
of your life
and wait there
patiently,
until the song
that is yours alone to sing
falls into your open cupped hands
and you recognize and greet it.
Only then will you know
how to give yourself
to the world
so worthy of rescue.[1]

MARTHA POSTLETHWAITE

BLESSED ARE THE CRAZY ONE

Here's to the crazy ones. The misfits. The rebels. The troublemakers. The round pegs in the square holes. The ones who see things differently. They're not fond of rules. And they have no respect for the status quo. You can quote them, disagree with them, glorify or vilify them. About the only thing you can't do is ignore them. Because they change things. They push the human race forward. And while some may see them as the crazy ones, we see genius. Because the people who are crazy enough to think they can change the world, are the ones who do.[1]

The script of 'Think Different', the TV advertising campaign for Apple (Computer) Inc, 1997–2002

Another script about thinking differently, delivered twenty centuries before, never caught the zeitgeist in the same way, but turned out to be even more influential. It was also about crazy ones, rebels and misfits. It was also about thinking differently. It was delivered by Jesus of Nazareth, and became known as the Sermon on the Mount, but it's more like a collection of one-liners and poems all located around a series of 'blessings':

Blessed are the poor in spirit, for theirs is the kingdom of heaven.
Blessed are those who mourn, for they will be comforted.
Blessed are the meek, for they will inherit the earth.
Blessed are those who hunger and thirst for righteousness, for they will be filled.
Blessed are the merciful, for they will receive mercy.
Blessed are the pure in heart, for they will see God.
Blessed are the peacemakers, for they will be called children of God.
Blessed are those who are persecuted for righteousness' sake, for theirs is the kingdom of heaven.
Blessed are you when people revile you and persecute you and utter evil against you on my account. Rejoice and be glad, for your reward is great in heaven[2]

Mahatma Gandhi – the man who led India to independence – kept these sayings, 'the Beatitudes', close to his heart. During negotiations with Lord Irwin, the Viceroy of India, Gandhi opened the Bible at the fifth chapter of Matthew's Gospel and said: 'When

HE REBELS, THE MISFITS

your country and mine shall get together on the teachings laid down by Christ in this Sermon on the Mount, we shall have solved the problems not only of our countries but those of the whole world.'[3]

Gandhi's methods in campaigning for independence for India inspired those of Martin Luther King Jr in the American Civil Rights movement. In *Stride Toward Freedom*, King wrote: 'Gandhi was probably the first person in history to lift the love ethic of Jesus above mere interaction between individuals to a powerful and effective social force on a large scale... in this Gandhian emphasis on love and nonviolence I discovered the method for social reform that I had been seeking... the only morally and practically sound method open to oppressed people in their struggle for freedom.'[4]

In this upside-down world that Jesus imagines, the blessings of life do not go to the rich and the powerful, to the famous and successful. Instead it's the poor and the meek who are blessed. Those who show mercy, those who seek righteousness, those who seek peace. Considering their poetic power

in inspiring people to change the course of history, the words of this ancient sermon often remain too intimidating or lacking in detail for most of us to take seriously. Gandhi said: 'I can tell you that in my humble opinion, what passes as Christianity is a negation of the Sermon on the Mount.'[5]

The novelist Kurt Vonnegut believed the Beatitudes were, regrettably, absent from US public life: '[They're] not exactly planks in a Republican platform. Not exactly George W. Bush, Dick Cheney, or Donald Rumsfeld stuff. For some reason, the most vocal Christians among us never mention the Beatitudes. But, often with tears in their eyes, they demand that the Ten Commandments be posted in public buildings. And of course that's Moses, not Jesus. I haven't heard one of them demand that the Sermon on the Mount, the Beatitudes, be posted anywhere. "Blessed are the merciful" in a courtroom? "Blessed are the peacemakers" in the Pentagon? Give me a break!'[6]

Blessed are the crazy ones, the rebels, the misfits. 'The people crazy enough to think they can change the world, are the ones who do.'[7]

97

Travel light

WHAT IF THIS ROAD?

What if this road, that has held no surprises
these many years, decided not to go
home after all; what if it could turn
left or right with no more ado
than a kite-tail? What if its tarry skin
were like a long, supple bolt of cloth,
that is shaken and rolled out, and takes
a new shape from the contours beneath?
And if it chose to lay itself down
in a new way; around a blind corner,
across hills you must climb without knowing
what's on the other side; who would not hanker
to be going, at all risks? Who wants to know
a story's end, or where a road will go?[1]

SHEENAGH PUGH

Who can predict the course of a life? Is it written in the stars? Is there a divine plan or is it blind fate? From where most of us are standing, it looks like we have to make it up as we go along. To play the hands we're dealt.

Our lives are the product of a huge multiplicity of factors: location, timing, culture, genes, upbringing, talent, education, peers, personality, chance, personal choice, and faith, or the lack of it.

Even though it's a cliché to say that life is a journey, it's true. You could call it a pilgrimage, except that pilgrims usually have a destination in mind: Mecca, Jerusalem, Santiago de Compostela...

Most of us have goals – short-term targets and long-term aspirations. Children may start off wanting to be doctors, astronauts, or *X Factor* winners, but often shift their focus as they begin to appreciate their abilities and limits.

We grow up with beliefs and codes of practice, inherited or absorbed from our family and background. But these tend to shift too, as life experience and education inform our understanding of the world. In late adolescence, especially, we can pass through what the philosopher Paul Ricoeur calls a 'desert of criticism',[2] in which we re-examine our beliefs, our ideas, even our identity.

But even when we reach the other side of that desert, having reshaped some of our ideas, most of us recognise that our conclusions are provisional. There are always new questions to ask. We may, for instance, lose a faith in God, or find one. Life surprises us because our journeys aren't mapped out ahead of time. Our decisions are subverted by events, or the grasping or spurning of opportunities. The person we fancy doesn't fancy us back. We fall ill. Someone offers us a job. We have a baby. As the Yiddish proverb puts it: 'Man makes plans and God laughs.'

We do our best to welcome the unexpected, to input the new coordinates and reset the sat nav. We travel on.

On each of our journeys we look for meaning and completeness. Quaker Richard Foster says about pilgrimage: 'The precise directions to somewhere are often awkward to find; and you're not sure quite why you came or what it was you're looking for. If you find it, or it finds you, words cannot easily convey what has happened but it becomes part of the journey that continues.'[3]

We make the journey up as we go along, taking strength and sustenance from what we pick up on the way. We can't see the whole picture, or find a unified theory of everything. We probably couldn't deal with it if we could. As the poet Olav H. Hauge wrote in 'Don't Give Me the Whole Truth':

don't give me the sky when I ask for light,
but give me a glint, a dewy wisp, a mote
as the birds bear water-drops from their
bathing
and the wind a grain of salt.[4]

We get clues on the direction to take from fellow travellers, from signposts, from our own internal compass. We pack for the journey, but our provisions are just that. Provisions. We learn to adapt – that it's best to travel light. Who wants to know, asks Sheenagh Pugh, where a story ends or where a road will go?

98

Let
go

Jochabed puts her baby Moses in a cute little crib, made of woven rushes, and watches him float off down the River Nile, where he is found by a lovely princess bathing in the water, daughter of the Pharoah. She plucks him from the water and brings him up as her own.

A storybook classic from the Bible. But why would a loving mother do that? Well, in this instance, because the baby's life was at risk after a decree had gone out in Egypt to kill all male newborns. Although Moses could have drowned or starved or been carried out to sea, if he was to have any chance of survival, Jochabed had to let him go.

It was a monumental risk and, in a sense, it's what parents have to do all the time. Raising children is a whole series of lettings go.

No one wants their kids to get hurt, yet the only way they'll grow is if they make mistakes – and get hurt. It's scary, but ultimately a parent has to remove the stabilisers from the bicycle. We let her teeter off – pedalling furiously, just to keep upright. For a moment, she flies. Then she meets the first corner. She swerves, topples, and ends up in a heap, with knees grazed and wheels spinning. Scared but exhilarated.

Letting children go means we may never see them again. That's their freedom. The same is true with our friends and siblings. We can't cling on to them either.

Possessiveness, over-protection, is stifling for everyone – it denies the other person their dignity. A mark of generosity is sharing our friends and families with other people. It's a risk: our friends might like them better than us. But often our circle of friends becomes bigger.

Every evening in Varanasi, India's holiest city, hundreds of people gather by the banks of the Ganges for the ceremony of the Fire Pujah, an offering to the female river deity. They place a lighted candle in a small leaf boat and launch their prayers, their hopes and dreams, then watch them bobble and twinkle out into the current. Then disappear into the night.

Jochabed took a chance and let Moses go. Later Moses took another, leading his people out of slavery, setting them on their long walk to freedom.

In her poem, 'The Language Issue', Nuala Ni Dhomhnaill says:

I place my hope on the water
in this little boat...
... only to have it borne hither and thither,
not knowing where it might end up...[1]

Love sometimes means giving a gentle push to a child, a friend, a precious idea. Then watching through your fingers, hoping and praying.

99

All you
need is
love

If I speak in the tongues of mortals and of angels, but do not have love, I am a noisy gong or a clanging cymbal. And if I have prophetic powers, and understand all mysteries and all knowledge, and if I have all faith, so as to remove mountains, but do not have love, I am nothing. If I give away all my possessions, and if I hand over my body so that I may boast, but do not have love, I gain nothing.

Love is patient; love is kind; love is not envious or boastful or arrogant or rude. It does not insist on its own way; it is not irritable or resentful; it does not rejoice in wrongdoing, but rejoices in the truth. It bears all things, believes all things, hopes all things, endures all things.

Love never ends. For now we see in a mirror, dimly, but then we will see face to face. Now I know only in part; then I will know fully, even as I have been fully known. And now faith, hope, and love abide, these three; and the greatest of these is love.

Abbreviated version of a letter from the early Christian leader, Paul.[1]

NOTES

Introduction
[1] Bono, in conversation with Martin Wroe, May, 2017.
[2] Leonard Cohen, 'Anthem', *The Future*, Columbia, 1992.

1. You don't have to choose between religion and spirituality
[1] Jon Stewart quoted in Michael Blitz, *Jon Stewart, A Biography*, ABC-CLIO, 2014.
[2] Lenny Bruce, quoted in John Cohen (ed.), *The Essential Lenny Bruce*, Bell, 1970.
[3] Barbara Brown Taylor, interview with Martin Wroe, *Church Times*, Aug 2013.
[4] Although this quote has been widely attributed to Garrison Keillor (on his radio show *Prairie Home Companion*), it most probably originated with the American evangelist Billy Sunday, see: John Eldridge Drewry (ed.), *Press, Radio, Television, Periodicals, Public Relations, and Advertising, as Seen through Institutes and Special Occasions of the Henry W. Grady School of Journalism*, University of Georgia Press, 1967.

2. Greet the day
[1] The hymn 'Morning Has Broken', words by Eleanor Farjeon, Oxford University Press, 1931.
[2] Ibid.
[3] Michael Leunig, 'The Day Before You', *The Age* (Melbourne), 17 June 2015.

3. Live the questions
[1] Rainer Maria Rilke, *Letters to a Young Poet, edited by Franz Xaver Kappus, 1934*, Letter 4, 1903.

4. Read the news
[1] Bill Gates, *The Annual Letter of Bill and Melinda Gates*, Bill and Melinda Gates Foundation, 2014.

5. Imagine it
[1] Yuval Noah Harari, *Sapiens: A Brief History of Mankind*, Harvill Secker, 2014.

6. Ride your luck
[1] '11 things that are more likely than winning the Lotto jackpot', *Independent*, 6 January 2016.
[2] Jim Al-khalili, www.humanism.org.uk (Humanists UK website).

7. Use the F-word
[1] Jill Saward, quoted in the *Guardian* 'Eve pays damages to rape victim', 14 Jan 2003.
[2] David Whyte, *Consolations: The Solace, Nourishment and Underlying Meaning of Everyday Words*, Many Rivers Press, 2015.
[3] Martin Luther King Jr, quoted in Coretta Scott King, *The Words of Martin Luther King*

Jr, Newmarket Press, 1983.
[4] Marina Cantacuzino, *The Forgiveness Project: Stories for a Vengeful Age*, Jessica Kingsley, 2015.
[5] Ibid.

8. Own up
[1] *Metro*, 'Self-service tills turn us into thieves', 29 January, 2014.

9. Stay friends
[1] Alden Nowlan, 'Great Things Have Happened', *Between Tears and Laughter: Selected Poems*, Anansi Press, 2004.
[2] 'Don't Walk in Front of Me', anonymous Hebrew folk song.
[3] Helen Keller, quoted in Joseph P. Lash, *Helen and Teacher: The Story of Helen Keller and Anne Sullivan Macy*, Delacorte, 1980.
[4] A. A. Milne, *The House at Pooh Corner*, Curtis Brown, Egmont, and Dutton, 1928.

10. Fear not
[1] Thich Nhat Hanh, *Fear: Essential Wisdom for Getting Through the Storm*, HarperOne, 2012.
[2] Michael Leunig, *A Common Prayer*, Collins Melbourne, 1990.

11. 'Do unto those downstream as you would have those upstream do unto you'
[1] Wendell Berry, *Citizenship Papers: Essays*, Counterpoint Press, 2003.

12. Stand still
[1] Seamus Heaney, 'St Kevin and the Blackbird', *Spirit Level*, Faber, 1996.
[2] William Blake, 'Auguries of Innocence', *The Complete Poems*, Penguin, 1977.
[3] Pablo Neruda, 'Keeping Quiet', *Extravagaria*, Jonathan Cape, 1972.

14. Write down the day
[1] Joan Didion, 'On Keeping a Notebook', *Slouching Towards Bethlehem*, Farrar, Straus and Giroux, 1968.
[2] Julia Cameron, *The Artist's Way: A spiritual path to higher creativity*, Jeremy P. Tarcher, 1992.

15. Listen to your life
[1] Frederick Buechner, *Now and Then: A Memoir of Vocation*, Harper San Francisco, 1991.

16. Be kind
[1] Jane Goodall, 'Being', in the series *The Secret Lives of Scientists and Engineers*, Sep 2014; https://www.youtube.com/watch?v=0Qu7Wn1mRYA.
[2] Dalai Lama, *An Appeal to the World: Ethics are More Important than Religion*, Benevento, 2016.

17. Trade stories
[1] Mary Oliver, 'The First Time Percy Came Back', *Dog Songs*, Penguin, 2015.
[2] Flannery O'Connor, *Mystery and Manners: Occasional Prose*, edited by Sally and Robert Fitzgerald, Faber & Faber, 1984.
[3] Philip Pullman, source unknown.
[4] Melanie Tem and Steve Rasnic Tem, *The Man on the Ceiling*, Wizards of the Coast, 2008.
[5] C. S. Lewis, *An Experiment in Criticism*, Cambridge University Press, 1961.
[6] Jeanette Winterson, *The Stone Gods*, Penguin, 2007.

18. Let your body do the talking
[1] Augustine of Hippo, Sermon 52:6.
[2] *The Nicene Creed*, AD 325.
[3] Tim Winton, *The Boy Behind the Curtain*, Hamish Hamilton, 2017.
[4] Mark Oakley, *The Splash of Words*, Canterbury Press, 2016.
[5] Mark 4.34
[6] Nicola Slee, 'The Power to Re-member', in *Swallowing a Fishbone: Feminists Debate Christianity*, edited by Daphne Hampson, SPCK, 1996.

19. Seize the day
[1] Rumi, 'The Guest House'.
[2] Margaret Atwood, 'Dear Americans...,' Twitter: Margaret E. Atwood@ MargaretAtwood, 9 November 2016.
[3] Bruce Cockburn, 'Waiting for a Miracle', *Anything Anytime Anywhere*, Carlin Music, 2002.
[4] Martin Luther King Jr, 'Baccalaureate sermon at the commencement exercises for Wesleyan University in Middletown', Connecticut, 1964.
[5] Cornel West, 'Commencement speech', Wesleyan University in Middletown, Connecticut, 1993.
[6] Solnit, 'The Arc of Justice'.
[7] Wink, *Powers That Be*.
[8] Psalm 23
[9] E. B. White, *Letters of Note: Correspondence Deserving a Wider Audience*, Canongate and Unbound, 2013.
[10] J. R. R. Tolkien, *The Lord of the Rings*, Allen and Unwin, 1954.

20. Trust your instinct
[1] Malcolm Gladwell, *Blink: The Power of Thinking Without Thinking*, Little Brown, 2005.
[2] Bono: *Bono on Bono: Conversations with Michka Assayas*, Hodder & Stoughton, 2006.
[3] Gladwell, *Blink*.
[4] Interview with Melvyn Bragg, *Third Way* magazine, Jun–Jul 1996, Vol. 19, no 5.
[5] Ibid.
[6] Ralph Waldo Emerson, *Essays, First Series*,

1841, Penguin, 2003.

21. Tune in
[1] George Herbert, 'Prayer (I), *The Complete Poetry of George Herbert*, Penguin, 2015.
[2] Anne Lamott, *Plan B: Further Thoughts on Faith*, Riverhead, 2005.
[3] Ann Lewin 'Disclosure', *Watching for the Kingfisher: Poems and Prayers*, Canterbury Press, 2009.

22. Make a habit of it
[1] Anne Lamott, *Bird by Bird: Some Instructions on Writing and Life*, Bantam, 1980.
[2] U. A. Fanthorpe, 'Atlas', *New and Collected Poems*, Enitharmon Press, 2010.
[3] Karen Armstrong, *The Spiral Staircase*, Anchor, 2004.
[4] Rabbi Chaim Stern, quoted in Rabbi Dennis S. Ross's blog 'On Being', 2 May 2015, https://onbeing.org/blog/ritual-is-poetry-in-action/.
[5] Aristotle, quoted in Will Durant, 'Summation of What He Said', *The Story of Philosophy: The Lives and Opinions of the World's Greatest Philosophers*, Simon & Schuster/Pocket Books, 1926.

23. Tell it like it is
[1] Salman Rushdie, *Defend the Right to Be Offended*, Open Democracy: Freethinking for the World, www.opendemocracy.net/faith-europe_islam/article_2331.jsp, 7 Feb 2005.
[2] Winston Churchill, interview with King-sley Martin, *New Statesman*, 7 Jan 1939.
[3] Alan Bennett, *Writing Home*, Faber & Faber, 1994.

24. Be more beastly
[1] Harari, *Sapiens*.
[2] Wendell Berry, 'The Peace of Wild Things', *The Selected Poems of Wendell Berry*, Counterpoint, 1998.
[3] Walt Whitman, 'Song of Myself', *Leaves of Grass*, 1855–92.

25. Pursue kindness
[1] *Daily Mirror*: Sammie Welch: Mum finds man who handed her heartwarming letter praising her parenting skills on train, 28 January 2015.
[2] Dalai Lama, An Appeal to the World, *Ethics Are More Important than Religion*, Benevento, 2016.

26. In the shelter of each other the people live
[1] Pádraig Ó Tuama 'In The Name', *In the Shelter*, Hodder, 2015.

28. Wake up
[1] Psalm 63.7
[2] Leonard Cohen, *Beautiful Losers*, Viking, 1966.

29. Know your place
[1] David Goodhart, *The Road to Somewhere:*

The Populist Revolt and the Future of Politics, C. Hurst & Co., 2017.
[2] Amanda Owen, interview with Malcolm Doney, *Church Times*, 22 Dec 2016.
[3] Ibid.
[4] Robert Macfarlane, *Landmarks*, Hamish Hamilton, 2015.

31. Let the music take you
[1] Douglas Adams, *The Salmon of Doubt*, Heinemann, 2002.
[2] David Bowie, CBS unaired interview, *60 Minutes*, 2003.
[3] Joseph Shabalala, 'A wise man keeps on singing', interview with David Thomas, *Daily Telegraph*, 27 Jun 2002.

32. 'Activism is my rent for living on this planet'
[1] Alice Walker, in Alice Walker and Prathiba Parar, *Alice Walker: Beauty in Truth*, Orion, 2013.

33. Take the road less travelled
[1] Bronnie Ware, *The Top Five Regrets of the Dying: A Life Transformed by the Dearly Departing*, Hay House, 2012.
[2] Raymond Carver, 'Gravy', *All of Us: The Collected Poems*, Knopf, 1996.
[3] George Saunders, 'George Saunders's Advice to Graduates', *The New York Times*, 31 Jul 2013, https://6thfloor.blogs.nytimes.com/2013/07/31/george-saunderss-advice-to-graduates/.

34. 'Remember you are dust'
[1] Guy Claxton, *The Wayward Mind: An Intimate History of the Unconscious*, Little, Brown, 2005.
[2] Ibid.
[3] William Wordsworth, 'Tintern Abbey', *Lyrical Ballads With a Few Other Poems*, Penguin, 2006.
[4] Nina Cassian, 'Temptation', translated by Brenda Walker and Andrew Deletanty, *Life Sentence: Selected Poems*, edited by William Jay Smith, Anvil Press, 1990.

35. Everybody hurts
[1] Alfred North Whitehead, *Process and Reality*, Free Press, 1978.
[2] REM, 'Everybody Hurts', *Automatic for the People*, Warner Bros, 1992.

36. Experience others
[1] J. K. Rowling acceptance speech at Harvard University honorary award ceremony, 2008, https://news.harvard.edu/gazette/story/2008/06/text-of-j-k-rowling-speech/.
[2] Maya Angelou, I *Know Why the Caged Bird Sings*, Virago Modern Classics, 2015,.
[3] Jonathan Franzen, *Farther Away*, Farrar Straus Giroux, 2012.

37. Be foolish
[1] Lewis Hyde, *The Gift: Imagination and the Erotic Life of Property*, Canongate, 2006.
[2] T. S. Eliot, 'Little Gidding', *The Four Quartets*, Faber & Faber, 1943.

38. There is no such thing as good grief
[1] John O'Donohue, 'For Grief', *Bless the Space Between Us: A Book of Blessings*, Doubleday, 2008.

40. 'This being human is a guest house'
[1] Jalaluddin Rumi, 'Guest House', *Selected Poems*, translated by Coleman Barks, Penguin, 2004.

41. Join the resistance
[1] Luis Enrique Mejía Godoy, 'Revenge', *Poets of the Nicaraguan Revolution*, edited and translated by Dinah Livingstone, Katabasis, 1993.
[2] Rosa Parks, cited in Donnie Williams and Wayne Greenhaw, *The Thunder of Angels: The Montgomery Bus Boycott and the People Who Broke the Back of Jim Crow*, Chicago Review Press, 2005.
[3] Walter Wink, *Engaging the Powers: Discernment and Resistance in a World of Domination*, Fortress Press, 1992.

42. Duty calls
[1] Thomas Merton, *No Man is an Island*, Harcourt, 1978.

43. Do good anyway
[1] Kent M. Keith, *The Silent Revolution: Dynamic Leadership in the Student Council*, Harvard Student Agencies, 1968.

44. God is Not a Christian (or Muslim, or Jew, or Buddhist, or Sikh, or Hindu, or agnostic, or atheist.)
[1] Genesis 1.27
[2] Harold S. Kushner, *The Book of Job: When Bad Things Happened to a Good Person*, Schocken Books, 2012.
[3] Desmond Tutu, *God Is Not a Christian and Other Provocations*, HarperOne, 2011.
[4] Ibid.

45. Keep the doubt
[1] Richard Holloway, *Leaving Alexandria: A Memoir of Faith and Doubt*, Canongate, 2012.
[2] John Keats, *The Complete Poetical Works and Letters of John Keats*, Cambridge Edition, Houghton Mifflin & Co, 1889.
[3] Holloway, *Leaving Alexandra*.
[4] Lamott, *Plan B*.

46. Faith…
[1] Richard Rohr, with Mike Morrell, *The Divine Dance: The Trinity and Your Transformation*, Whitaker House, 2016.
[2] Brené Brown, *Rising Strong*, Spiegel and Grau, 2015.

47. Hope…
[1] Walter Wink, *The Powers That Be*, Bantam, 1998.
[2] Rebecca Solnit, 'The Arc of Justice and the Long Run: Hope, history and unpredictability', *Huffington Post*, 22 Feb 2014, http://www.huffingtonpost.com/rebecca-solnit/the-arc-of-justice-and-the-

long-run_b_4494297.html.

48. Love...
[1] Fyodor Dostoevsky, *The Brothers Karamazov*, translated by Constance Garnett, M. Dent & Sons, Everyman's Library, 1950.

49. How and Why Are Different Questions
[1] Genesis 1.
[2] Richard Dawkins, 'Lecture from the Nullifidian', Dec 1994, www.richarddawkins.net.
[3] Albert Einstein, 'Letter to Eric Gutkind, 1954', *Letters of Note*, ed. Sean Usher, Canongate and Unbound, 2013.
[4] Stephen Jay Gould, *Rocks of Ages: Science and Religion in the Fullness of Li*fe, Ballantine, 2002.
[5] Jonathan Sacks, *The Great Partnership: God, Science and the Search for Meaning*, John Murray Press an imprint of Hodder & Stoughton, 2011.

50. Only remember
[1] Hymn 'Only Remembered', words by Horatius Bonar (1870), music by Ira Sankey (1891).
[2] Ibid.

51. Show compassion
[1] Karen Armstrong, *Twelve Steps to a Compassionate Life*, Bodley Head, 2011.
[2] Ibid.
[3] 'The Charter for Compassion', this statement, written by Karen Armstrong, is the centrepiece of Charter for Compassion, a charitable organisation, www.charterforcompassion.org.

52. Unplug yourself
[1] Radiohead, *Kid A*, Parlophone, 2000.
[2] Anne Lamott, Facebook post, 4 August 2015.

53. Shake on it
[1] Pádraig Ó Tuama,'Shaking Hands', *Sorry For Your Troubles*, Canterbury Press, 2013.

54. Bear witness
[1] Arundhati Roy, *War Talk*, South End Press, 2003.
[2] Oliver Sacks, *The Writers' Almanac*, 9 Jul 2016. https://writersalmanac.org/note/july-9-2016-birthday-oliver-sacks/.
[3] Elie Wiesel, National Public Radio PR obituary, 2 Jul 2016, http://www.npr.org/sections/thetwo-way/2016/07/02/166184644/elie-wiesel-holocaust-survivor-and-nobel-laureate-dies-at-87.
[4] Mahatma Gandhi, source unknown.

55. I am because you are
[1] Kurt Vonnegut, *Deadeye Dick*, Delacorte, 1982 (though the phrase had been in circulation since the 1960s).
[2] 'Brief Meaning of African Word UBUNTU', Ubuntu Women Institute USA, 24 Jan 2012.
[3] Desmond Tutu, *No Future Without Forgiveness*, Rider & Co., 1999.

56. Fail again. Fail better
[1] James Dyson, 'Failure Doesn't Suck', interview with Chuck Salter, *Fast Company* magazine, 5 January 2007.
[2] 2 Corinthians 12.9.
[3] Mario Livi, *Project Syndicate*, Feb 2014, https://www.project-syndicate.org/commentary/mario-livio-emphasizes-the-critical-role-of-mistakes-in-driving-scientific-progress?barrier=accessreg.
[4] Dyson, 'Failure Doesn't Suck'.
[5] Neil Gaiman, 'Keynote address to the University of the Arts in Philadelphia', May 2012, https://www.uarts.edu/neil-gaiman-keynote-address-2012.
[6] Samuel Beckett, *Worstward Ho*, Grove, 1983.

57. Sex it up
[1] Steven Pinker, *How the Mind Works*, W. W. Norton, 1997.
[2] Bruce Cockburn, 'The Coldest Night of the Year', *Mummy Dust*, True North, 1981.
[3] John O'Donohue, *Anam Cara*, Bantam, 1997.

58. Live with the unknown
[1] Barbara Brown Taylor, *Learning to Walk in the Dark*, Canterbury Press, 2014.

59. Say a little prayer
[1] Sister Wynona Carr, 'Operator, Operator', 1954.

60. It is solved by walking
[1] Stephen and Ondrea Levine, *Who Dies? An Investigation of Conscious Living and Conscious Dying*, Doubleday, 1989.
[2] Talking Heads, 'The Road to Nowhere', *Little Creatures*, Warner Bros, 1985.
[3] Douglas Adams, *The Hitchhiker's Guide to the Galaxy*, Pan, 1979.
[4] R. S. Thomas, 'The Bright Field', *R. S. Thomas, Collected Poems 1945–1990*, Dent, 1993.
[5] Ludwig Wittgenstein, 'Journal entry 8 July 1916', *Notebooks 1914–1916*, Blackwells, 1961.

61. 'Never forget that justice is what love looks like in public'
[1] Cornel West, interview with David Shuster, 24 February 2014, American Aljazeera, http://america.aljazeera.com/watch/shows/talk-to-al-jazeera/interviews-and-more/2014/2/24/cornel-west-talkstodavidshuster.html.

62. Question everything
[1] Matt Haig, *The Humans*, Canongate, 2013.

63. Take a day off
[1] Thich Nhat Hanh, *The Pocket Thich Nhat Hanh*, Shambhala, 2012.

[2] Ovid, source unknown.
[3] Maya Angelou, *Wouldn't Take Nothing for My Journey Now*, Virago, 1995.

64. 'Kiss the ground'
[1] Jalaluddin Rumi, 'Kiss the Ground', *Selected Poems*, translated by Coleman Barks, Penguin, 2004.

65. Find your way home
[1] Mahmoud Darwish, interview with Adam Shatz, *The New York Times*, 'A Poet's Palestine as a Metaphor', 22 Dec 2001.
[2] Diane Ackerman, PowellsBooks.Blog, interview with Jill Owens, 18 Sep 2007. http://www.powells.com/post/interviews/diane-ackerman.
[3] Walter Brueggemann, *Cadences of Home: Preaching Among Exiles*, Westminster John Knox Press, 2007.
[4] Darwish, *New York Times*.
[5] Martin Buber, quoted by Joseph Campbell in 1970 lecture, 'Manhattan', Cooper Union, http://www.huffingtonpost.com/derek-beres/the-every-day-religion-of_b_580764.html.

66. When you fail – come clean
[1] Francis Spufford, *Unapologetic: Why, despite everything, Christianity can still make surprising emotional sense*, Faber & Faber, 2012.
[2] Ibid.

67. Be enchanted
[1] Mircea Eliade, *Myth of the Eternal Return: Cosmos and History (Works of Mircea Eliade)*, Princeton University Press, 1971.
[2] Marcus Borg, *Convictions: How I Learned What Matters Most*, HarperOne, 2014.
[3] William James, *Varieties of Religious Experience: A Study in Human Nature*, Longmans Green & Co, 1901.
[4] Ibid.
[5] Emily Dickinson, 'Some Keep the Sabbath Going to Church', *The Poems of Emily Dickinson*, ed R. W. Franklin, Harvard University Press, 1999.

68. Pay attention
[1] David Foster Wallace, *This is Water: Some thoughts, delivered on a significant occasion, about living a compassionate life*, Little Brown and Company, 2009.
[2] Ibid.
[3] Wendell Berry, *Life is a Miracle*, Counterpoint Press, 1985.
[4] Patrick Kavanagh, 'The Parish and the Universe', in *Collected Prose*, MacGibbon & Kee, 1967.
[5] Macfarlane, *Landmarks*.
[6] Wallace, *This is Water*.

69. Expect the unexpected
[1] R. S. Thomas 'Pilgrimages', *Collected Poems 1945–1990*, J. M. Dent, 1993.
[2] R. S. Thomas, 'Via Negativa', *Collected Poems 1945–1990*, J. M. Dent, 1993.
[3] George Steiner, *Real Presences*, University

of Chicago Press, 1989.
[4] Steve Turner,'Spiritus', *Poems: The Best of Steve Turner*, Lion Publishing, 2002

70. Love is a verb
[1] 'All You Need is Love', John Lennon and Paul McCartney, Parlophone, Capitol, 1967.

71. Come to Jesus
[1] Mark 3.21.

72. 'Make big decisions slowly and small decisions fast'
[1] James Martin, *The Jesuit Guide to Everything*, Harper Collins, 2014.
[2] Anthony Wilson, 'When the Holy Spirit Danced with Me in the Kitchen', *Full Stretch*, Worple Press, 2006.

73. See the entire universe in the meal you're about to eat
[1] Martin Luther King Jr, 'A Christmas Sermon on Peace', in James Melvin Harper (ed.), *A Testament of Hope, The Essential Writings of Martin Luther King Jr*, 1991.
[2] Bart Simpson, 'Two cars in every garage and three eyes on every fish', *The Simpsons* Season Two, Episode 7F01, 1 Nov 1990.
[3] Robert Burns, 'Selkirk Grace', *The Complete Poems and Songs of Robert Burns*, Waverley Books, 2011.

74. Disorientate yourself
[1] Psalm 137.
[2] Nick Cave, *The Complete Lyrics 1978-2001*, Penguin, 2001.
[3] Bono, *The Book of Psalms*, Canongate, 1999.
[4] Psalm 23.

75. Thanks will be enough
[1] Edna Healey, *The Independent*, Obituary, 23 July 2010.
[2] W. S. Merwin, 'Thanks', *Migration: New and Selected Poems*, Copper Canyon Press, 2005.
[3] Ibid.

76. Get religion
[1] REM, 'Losing my Religion', *Out of Time*, Warner Bros, 1991.
[2] Sunday Assembly, www.sundayassembly.com.
[3] Linda Woodhead, *Why No Religion is the New Religion*, British Academy Lecture, 19 Jan 2016.
[4] Alain de Botton, *Religion for Atheists: A Non-believer's Guide to the Uses of Religion*, Signal, 2012.

77. Make yourself up
[1] Wendell Berry, *Jayber Crow*, Counterpoint Press, 2000.
[2] Po Bronson, *What Should I Do with My Life?*, Random House, 2003.
[3] Caitlin Moran, *How to Build a Girl*, Ebury Press, 2014.

78. Shhhh. . .
[1] 'Just think: The challenges of the disengaged mind', Professor Timothy Wilson, *Science*, Vol. 345, Issue 6192, 4 Jul 2014.
[2] Michael Palin, *'Fifty Things to Do in a Church*, Diocese of London', 16 Aug 2016, *www.london.anglican.org/articles/50-things-church*.
[3] Spufford, *Unapologetic*.

79. Share this bread
[1] Margaret Atwood, 'All Bread', *Selected Poems II: Poems Selected and New 1976-1986*, Oxford University Press, 1986.
[2] Ibid.

80. Become your best self
[1] David Brooks, *The Road to Character*, Allen Lane, 2015.

81. Take the overview
[1] Chris Hedges, 'What every person should know about war', *The New York Times*, 6 Jul 2003.
[2] Frank White, *The Overview Effect: Space Exploration and Human Evolution*, Houghton Mifflin, 1987.
[3] Edgar Mitchell, in White, *Overview Effect*.
[4] Nicole Stott in Planetary Collective film, *Overview*: planetarycollective.com/overviewthemovie.com/.
[5] Ron Garan, in film *Overview*.
[6] William Anders, in film *Overview*.

82. Light a candle
[1] *Christian Herald and Seaman's Magazine*, Volume 8, 1821.
[2] Henri Matisse, *Henri Matisse: The Cut Outs*, Tate Publishing, 2014.
[3] Michael Leunig, *When I Talk to You: A cartoonist talks to God*, Andrews McMeel, 2006.

83. Practise resurrection
[1] Wendell Berry, Manifesto: *The Mad Farmer Liberation Front*, Counterpoint, 1973.
[2] Richard Rohr, *From the Immortal Diamond: The search for our true self*, Crossroad Publishing Company, 2013.

84. Put down roots
[1] Louis de Bernières, *Captain Corelli's Mandolin*, Harvill Secker, 1994.

85. Live your way into a new kind of thinking
[1] Ann Morisy, *Journeying Out*, Continuum, 2004.
[2] Henri Nouwen, *Life of the Beloved: Spiritual Living in a Secular World*, Crossroad Publishing, 1992.

86 Let evening come
[1] Leonardo DiCaprio, interview with Simon Mayo, BBC Radio 5 Live, 5 Jan 2016.
[2] Denise Levertov, 'Variations on a Theme by Rilke', *New and Selected Poems*, Bloodaxe Books, 2003.

87. 'Everybody worships'

[1] Wallace, *This is Water*.

88. Lighten up
[1] Desmond Tutu, *An African Prayer Book*, Bantam, 1998.

89. You'll never walk alone
[1] Jane Siberry, 'The Valley', *Bound by the Beauty*, Duke St Records/Reprise, 1989.
[2] Michael Donaghy, 'The Present', *Dances Learned Last Night: Poems 1975–1995* Picador, 2000.

90. Take the journey with the dead guy
[1] Psalm 90. 10.
[2] Thomas Lynch, *The Undertaking: Life studies from the dismal trade*, Vintage, 1997.

91. Replay the day
[1] Annie Dillard, *The Writing Life*, Harper Collins, 1989.

93. Live in the long now
[1] Brian Eno, The Long Now Foundation, *http://longnow.org*.
[2] Isaiah 40.3.

94. Believe it or not
[1] Belief-O-Matic, www.beliefnet.com.
[2] Spufford, *Unapologetic*.
[3] Borg, *Convictions*.

95. 'Create a clearing'
[1] Martha Postlethwaite, 'Clearing'.

96. Blessed are the crazy ones, the rebels, the misfits
[1] 'Think Different', Apple_Inc., 1997.
[2] Matthew 5.
[3] Mahatma Gandhi, in Robert Ellsberg (ed.), *Gandhi on Christianity*, Orbis, 1991.
[4] Martin Luther King Jr, *Stride Towards Freedom*, Harper, 1958.
[5] Gandhi, *Gandhi on Christianity*.
[6] Kurt Vonnegut, *A Man Without a Country: A memoir of life in George W. Bush's America*, Bloomsbury, 2006.
[7] Ibid.

97. Travel light
[1] Sheenagh Pugh, 'What if This Road', *Id's Hospit*, Seren Books, 1997.
[2] Paul Ricoeur, *The Symbolism of Evil*, translated by Emerson Buchanan, Beacon, 1969.
[3] Richard Foster, *Celtic Daily Prayer: Book One*, William Collins, 2015.
[4] Olav H. Hauge, 'Don't Give Me the Whole Truth', *Leaf-Huts and Snow-Houses: Selected poems*, translated by Robert Fulton, Anvil Press, 2003.

98. Let go
[1] Nuala Ni Dhomhnaill, 'The Language Issue', *Pharaoh's Daughter*, translated by © Paul Muldoon, Gallery Press, 1990.

99. All you need is love
[1] 1 Corinthians 13.

COPYRIGHT ACKNOWLEDGEMENTS

surprising emotional sense, © Francis Spufford, 2012, reproduced with permission of Faber & Faber.

95. 'Create a clearing'
'Clearing', © Martha Postlethwaite, reproduced with permission of Martha Postlethwaite.

96. Blessed are the crazy ones, the rebels, the misfits
Extract from *Stride Towards Freedom*, © Martin Luther King Jr, 1958, reproduced with permission of The King Estate; Extract from *A Man Without a Country: A memoir of life in George W. Bush's America*, © Kurt Vonnegut, 2006, reproduced with permission of Bloomsbury.

97. Travel light
'Don't Give Me the Whole Truth', © Olav H. Hauge and Robert Fulton, 2003, reproduced with permission of Anvil Press; 'What if This Road', © Sheenagh Pugh, 1997, reproduced with permission of Seren Books.

98. Let go
'The Language Issue', © Nuala Ni Dhomhnaill and Paul Muldoon, 1990, reproduced with permission of Paul Muldoon.

IMAGE CREDITS

THANKS

... to the several hundred people who have tied up their good money for a year or two in the hope that this book would be worth the wait. It's a relatively humiliating experience to hold out an online begging bowl, while trying to build the budget to publish a book you have a hunch someone out there might be waiting to read. Thank you for trusting us to make this book happen.

Lifelines was a long time in the gestation and has too many parents to identify – but our partners, Meryl and Meg, can't go unmentioned. In the years the two of us have worked together as friends and writers, there have been particular communities and cohorts of friendships that have figured strongly in its conception.

It's hard to underestimate the role of an annual arts festival called Greenbelt, which for forty odd years has been trying to suggest a more elusive, less prescriptive, description of living inside one of the great faith stories – one distinct from the busted flush of institutional religion.

Over several years in the 1980s and 90s there was a long-running weekly hang-out on Tuesday nights called Crouch End United, when a crowd of us showed up after work to argue about art, or theology, or politics, or fiction – 'iron sharpening iron' as the book of Proverbs puts it, 'one person sharpening the wits of another'.

We each, at different times, edited a magazine called *STRAIT*, exploring art and culture through the lens of faith, and later edited, together, *Developments*, this time for the UK Government's Department for International Development, which gave us the chance to spend time in developing countries, to put our own country into a different context, and to hear from people living inside different cultural, economic and religious traditions.

While we both started out in what used to be called non-conformism, we eventually gravitated towards a rickety township called the Church of England. Here, we were lucky to find a crowd of people in a small north London community named after St Luke, who were also trying to re-imagine their faith stories and working them out as a kind of provisional life experiment.

We dreamed up this book thinking we might come up with ninety-five new 'theses' to mark the 500th anniversary of the original ninety-five, pinned on a church door by Martin Luther and inadvertently sparking the revolution that became known as the Reformation. The American writer Phyllis Tickle suggested that such reformations come with a half-millennium cycle, a great spring clean of institutional religion which in *The Great Emergence*, she called 'The 500-Year Rummage Sale'.

Around about now we're experiencing the latest, which may explain why – if you're interested in the geography of spirituality – the early part of the twenty-first century seems a kind of liminal place, where one tidy version of faith is slowly being superseded by something altogether more untidy, and open-ended: one that welcomes questions more than answers. This book is just one of the many wobbly trestle tables in the great village hall of history, as human life potters around looking for some kind of affordable hope to carry them through another few days.

We missed the Luther anniversary but maybe *Lifelines* can provide what the novelist Tim Winton calls 'a steadying of nerves for the onward journey'.

Malcolm Doney, Martin Wroe, April 2018

(Special thanks to Anna Lawrence whose heroic work seeking and finding the lost permissions should not go unsung and to Simon Gunn, for whom the word 'designer' falls well short of his role in making *Lifelines* look so good. And also to the good people of Unbound, in particular Anna Simpson and Scott Pack, our editorial midwives.)

SUPPORTERS

Unbound is a new kind of publishing house. Our books are funded directly by readers. This was a very popular idea during the late eighteenth and early nineteenth centuries. Now we have revived it for the internet age. It allows authors to write the books they really want to write and readers to support the books they would most like to see published.

The names listed below are of readers who have pledged their support and made this book happen. If you'd like to join them, visit www.unbound.com.

Esther Addley
David Alderdice
Angela Allen
Billie & Seamus
   Anderson
Fraser Anderson
Morey Andrews
Anna Arthur
Ade Ashaye
Dayo Ashaye
Pat Ashworth
Bobby Baker
Jenny Baker
Susannah Baker
Peter Banks
Peter Barrett
Emma and Paul Bennett
Matt Bere
Rachel Blackamore
Lucy Blair
Mark Blair
Sharon Blankson
Peter Bone
Russell Boulter
Jaime Martinez
   Bowness

Paul Bowring
Samantha Bowring
Mark Brennan
Kester Brewin
Andy Brookes
Rosemary Brown
Tim Brown
Richard Bull
David Burgess
Steve Butler
Bernadette Cagnoni
Lois Cameron
Tony Cant
Oliver Carruthers
Scott Casey
Andrew Caspari
Geraldine Casswell
Iain Cathcart
J Brian Celler
Chalky
Gordon Charlton
Caroline Chartres
Jonathan and Alison
   Clark
A Clayton
Libby Coats

Anthony Collins
Tina Cooke
Philip Coombes
Ian Coombs
Sue Cooper
Mary Corfield
Peter Cotton
Roselyn Crane
Geoff Crawford
Andy Cribb
Phil Critchlow
Philip Crocker
Kath Cubitt
Liz Curran
Mike Dark & John
   Blowers
Brian Davidson
Dr Peter Davies
John Davies
Kathryn Davies
Mark Dean
Tim Dean
Chris Doney
Ellie Doney
Lewis Doney
Norman Doney

Amos Doornbos
David Downing
John Drake
Brian Draper
Peter Driver
Fraser Dyer
Harry Edwards
Laurence Edwards
Ellie Elliott
Stuart Elliott
David Emmerson
Craig Evans
Martin Evans
Jonathan Evens
Jake Fairnie
Cathleen Falsani
David Felten
Mary Fitzmaurice
Arthur Fogel
Rob Francis
Ann Frank
Nazar Georgis
Rosa Gindele
Peter & Sheena
    Ginnings
Darren Goddard
Mark Godson
Adrian Goodall
Aaron Govern
Fiona Green
Ann Griese
Tabitha Griffiths
Simon Gunn
Becky Hall
Simon Hall
Stu Hallam
Luke Halls
Dave Hancock
Paul Handley
Zane Hannan
Elizabeth Hanvey
Fionan Hanvey

TJ Harkin
Jim Harris
Andy & Sibs Harrison
Peter Haughton
Philippa Haughton
Tim Haughton
Stephen Heard
Katherine Hedderly
Abi Hewitt
Ben Hewitt
Garth and Gill Hewitt
Gareth Higgins
Derek Hill
David Hillyer
Lucy C Hirst
Crispin Holland
Paul Hollingum
Mark Holmes
Daniel Hulls
Alan Ivory
J C
Lisa Jackman
Caroline Jackson
Gary Jermyn
Harvey Jessop
Phil Johnstone
Brian Jolley
Hugh Jones
James Jones
Simon Joe Jones
Martyn Joseph
Graham Judd
Harry Kantas
Miriam Kaufmann
April Keech
Dan Kieran
Andrew Knowles
Hannah Kowszun
Ross Kuehne
Sherry Lawrence
Alf & Mary Lawson
Simon Lawson

Brian Leckey
Carl Lee
Luke Leighfield
Ayla Lepine
Gillian and Jake Lever
Tamasin Little
Dave Lovering-Roddis
Joan Lyon
Susan Mactavish
Geoff Maddock
Abdul-Rehman Malik
David Mansfield
David Marsh
Janet Marshall
Jo Marshall
Mike Martin
Rob Martin
Mary & David
Lucy Matthew
Chris Matthews
Graham Maule
Simon Mayo
The Mayos (Dorking
    branch)
Niamh McCarthy
Sarah McCartney
Neil McCormick
Steven McEwan
Matt McGee
Mark McKee
Shona McLeod
Dave Mellows
Peter Melrose
Nick Mercer
Arun Midha
John Mitchinson
Les Moir
Glynis Moor
Cole Moreton
Charles Morris
Peter Mortimer
Alison Motley

Brenda Motley
Carlo Navato
Tim Neufeld
Adrian Newman
Paul Newton
John Noble
Barbar Nokes
Daniel Northam Jones
Paul Northup
Pádraig Ó Tuama
Debbie O'Brien
Eryl O'Day
Mark Oakley
Martine Oborne
Par Olsson
Scott Pack
Hilary Painter
Helen Parkyns
Veronica Pasteur
Ruth Peacock
Adrian Pearson
Michelle Pearson
The Pengelly-Becketts
Alan Perry
Tom Peryer
Simon Peyton Jones
Edward Pillar
Ruth Pimenta
George Pitcher
Sue and Simon Plater
Lorraine Pointon
Justin Pollard
Arthur Pooley
Andy Powell
David Pratt
Alistair Prentice
Jeff Procter-Murphy
Harry Rae
Lisa Rainier
Adrian Reith
Angela Reith
Judy Reith

Mike & Rose Riddell
Joanna Rivard
Dave Roberts
Rhian Roberts
Jean Roberts for the
    Copelands
Andy Robertson
Jane Roe
Russell Rook
Chris Rose
Ricky Ross
Sarah Rowe
Kathy Rudiger
Andy Russell
Dan Russell
Jonathan Rust
Beverley Sage
David Sceats
Vera Schuster Beesley
Ali Seal
Jonna Sercombe
Andrew and Rosie
    Sheldon
Rupert Shortt
Anna Sillett
Danielle Silverman
Vera Sinton
Craig Smillie
Martin Smith
Morleigh Steinberg
Elisabeth and Aidan
    Stewart
James & Kari Stewart
Hagen Stroh
Steve Summers
Debbie Symes
Andrew Tate
Mark Tauber
Sally Taylor
Steve & Debbie Taylor
Raymond Tetz
Jemima Thackray

Richard Thomas
Andy Thornton
Ed Thornton
Steve Tomkins
Dave Tomlinson
Treatment Limited
Rachel Turner
James Tweed
Dave Tyler
Sophia Ufton
Cara Usher
Anna Vaught
Kevin Veloso
Bruno Villers
Rachel Wakefield
Michael Wakelin
Dave Walker
Joe Walker
Denise Ward
Jonathan Ware
Katie and Emily Watson
Brian Whelan and
    Wendy Roseberry
Simon White
Dean & Emma Willars
Michael Williams
Anthony Wilson
Kurt Wilson
Emma Winterleigh
Jeremy Woodham
George Wrigley
Enid Wroe
Grace Wroe
John & Joanne Wroe
Martin Wroe
Mathew, Sarah, Daniel
    & Thomas Wroe
Meg Wroe
Paul Wroe
Wesley Wroe
Mark Yaconelli
Veronica Zundel